CHURCH OFFICER AND COMMITTEE GUIDEBOOK,

REVISED

JAMES A. SHEFFIELD

TIM J. HOLCOMB

ISBN: 0-7673-1953-2

This book is the resource for course LS-0096 in the subject area Leadership and Skill
Development in the Christian Growth Study Plan.

Dewey Decimal Classification: 254
Subject Heading: CHURCH COMMITTEES//CHURCH ADMINISTRATION

To order additional copies of this resource: write LifeWay Church Resources Customer
Service; One LifeWay Plaza; Nashville, TN 37234-0113; fax order to (615) 251-5933;
phone toll free (800) 458-2772; ORDER ONLINE at *www.lifeway.com;*
or VISIT the LifeWay Christian Store serving you.

Printed in the United States of America

Leadership and Adult Publishing
LifeWay Church Resources
One LifeWay Plaza
Nashville, TN 37234-0175

Contents

Chapter 1   Why Church Officers and Committees Are Needed 4

Chapter 2   Determining a Church's Committee Structure 7

Chapter 3   Duties of Church Officers................ 12

Chapter 4   Duties of Permanent Committees 16

Chapter 5   Duties of Special Committees and Councils 28

Chapter 6   Coordinating Church Committee Work 36

Chapter 7   Committee Training and Orientation 41

Chapter 8   The Role of the Chairperson 44

Chapter 9   Effective Committee Work 52

              Personal Learning Activities 61

              Suggestions for the Teacher................... 63

Chapter 1

Why Church Officers and Committees Are Needed

A church committee is a group of persons assigned specific tasks by the congregation to assist the church in planning its program, managing its resources, and governing its life and work.

Church officers are assigned administrative tasks that are usually performed by one person. However, some churches designate trustees as church officers. The difference in this type of group and a committee is that trustees deal with legal matters only. Trustees are usually not a decision-making or planning group.

Other church officers include treasurer, church clerk, and moderator. The duties of church officers are listed in chapter 3. Committee duties are listed in chapters 4 and 5.

Each church has responsibility for handling all of its administrative work. However, if a church tried to handle all of the details during a business meeting, the meeting would become chaotic. Consequently, most churches delegate to church officers and committees the responsibilities for planning, making recommendations, and managing the resources.

But why do churches need committees and officers? What benefits are derived from churches using officers and committees?

The moderator calls the congregation to order for the October business meeting. The purpose of the business meeting has been announced as budget planning time. After the moderator calls the meeting to order, he opens the session by saying, "It is now time to plan the budget for the new year. Do I hear recommendations from the floor?"

An elderly person stands and says, "I've noticed our buildings are not clean. I don't think we have enough janitorial staff to do a thorough job. I move we hire two additional custodians."

Someone quickly replies, "We can't do that. We can't afford it. We just need to get some volunteers to do the extra cleaning required."

A third person states, "Don't count on too many people to volunteer. We can't get volunteers to teach Sunday School, much less clean buildings."

Another person rises to state an opinion. "We have too many people on our payroll. I object to adding people to our staff. Besides, our buildings are fine."

Do you get the picture? If this kind of discussion were to take place on the floor of the business meeting without prior planning and discussion in appropriate committees, the result would be disastrous.

The pastor has just resigned. The chairperson of the deacons steps to the platform and says, "Since we no longer have a pastor, I recommend that every member of this congregation serve on the pastor search committee so we can find a replacement for our pastor as soon as possible."

Ridiculous? Yes, this would certainly create confusion and problems. Good judgment would indicate the necessity of appointing a small group to search for and recommend a new pastor to the congregation.

What would happen in a church if no one were charged with the responsibility of worker enlistment? Can you imagine the scene when new workers were needed to start the new church year? What confusion there would be if no one in the church took the responsibility for seeing that volunteer workers were available.

Another area that needs a committee is the building and grounds a church owns and operates. What if no one were charged with the responsibility for seeing that facilities are maintained? The situation would be deplorable. Much of the Lord's money would be wasted if churches did not set into operation some kind of preventive maintenance program. A church property and space committee can and should do the necessary studies and projections to ensure that the church is a good steward of the facilities and properties it owns.

What would a church do for historical records without a church clerk? How would the church be able to refer to decisions if no minutes were kept of business meetings? Who would have responsibility for gathering statistics for the Annual Church Profile if the church had no clerk?

Illustrations abound. The need for administrative services such as officers and committees cannot be denied. Therefore, a church needs to make sure it does the best job possible in using church officers and committees to help the church be and do what God desires.

Do church officers and committees provide benefits for a church? The illustrations given above say yes. A church will realize the following benefits if church officers and committees are used wisely.

Save time in church business meetings. A committee that has done its homework and has prepared reports and recommendations will save time in a business meeting. A committee report and recommendations that are presented with full explanations and written and/or visual helps usually answer most questions before they are asked.

Utilize knowledge and special skills of church members. By placing people who understand building needs, building structure, and building maintenance on the property and space committee, a church will benefit from the expertise of these people. But these committee members will also benefit from using their skills. They will grow in their commitment to the Lord. They will feel useful and will feel they are making a contribution.

Provide opportunity to develop members. A church has the responsibility to help its members mature as Christians. Allowing people to serve as church officers or committee members helps them grow and mature as church members and Christians. However, be careful about placing inactive members on a committee with the hope that they will become active. This approach rarely works.

Discover effective ways for carrying on the work of the church. A church needs to be constantly looking for more effective methods of carrying out its administrative responsibilities. Church officers and committee members who are committed to their tasks will often find more effective and efficient ways to administer the work of a church.

Churches may use a finance committee to develop a strong set of financial policies and procedures. Wise policies and procedures help them remain financially sound and eliminate many routine problems in administering their budgets. Committees can make a difference!

Provide opportunities for detailed study of specific problems. The last church I served believed it was time for our church to enter the computer age. The finance committee conducted an in-depth study of computer programs available for churches. The committee interviewed several companies that provided computer programs and hardware. When the committee was ready to make its recommendations, the church accepted the proposals without much discussion and limited questions. Why? Because the committee had done its homework and answered most of the questions. Also, by having a committee do this kind of study, the staff members involved were not put on the spot. It was a committee recommendation, not a staff proposal.

Provide opportunities to reconcile divergent viewpoints. Many times a church has to consider programs or decisions that will provoke discussion and, sometimes, dissension. In these cases, committees provide the opportunity to deal with the differing viewpoints in committee meetings and not on the floor of the church business meeting.

Conclusion

Church officers and committees are necessary. The other option—no committees or officers—does not appear to be a logical choice. Confusion and problems will occur if a church chooses not to have committees and officers.

The other side of the coin is that some churches have abused the committee process. The saying, "If you want to kill an idea or suggestion, form a committee to study it," is familiar to all of us. Churches have also abused the committee structure by starting committees but never deleting them after their work is completed. Churches that have too many committees overlap and duplicate work. Many of these abuses have given committee work a bad name. But committees are necessary and play an important role in helping a church run smoothly and stay focused on its mission.

Some churches need to quit making fun of committees and get serious about making committee work effective. This book can provide suggestions and help for your church if it really sees the need for committees.

Chapter 2

DETERMINING A CHURCH'S COMMITTEE STRUCTURE

How many committees should a church have? Which committees are valid? How long should a committee remain a permanent committee? To whom should committees report? How can a church bring its committee structure up-to-date?

These and other questions will be answered in this chapter. Keep in mind, however, that one book cannot cover all the possibilities for every church. The suggestions provided in this chapter are guidelines only.

Kinds of Committees

A Children's Sunday School department director asked one Sunday, "What different kinds of Bibles do we have today." A child responded quickly, "Red, black, white, brown."

In response to the question, what kinds of committees should a church have? you might get a similar answer, such as "large, small, medium-sized."

Most churches will discover the merits of identifying committees in one of two ways: *regular* or *permanent* and *special* or *temporary*. Every time a new committee is formed, the decision should be made about the kind of committee it is. All existing committees should be assigned regular/permanent status or special/temporary status.

A *permanent* committee is assigned duties that are ongoing. The duties will be performed indefinitely.

Committees that can terminate at a specific point in time should be classified special or temporary. For example, a committee formed to write a constitution and bylaws could be a temporary committee. This type of committee has a definite assignment that will be completed once the constitution and bylaws are adopted by the church.

Another type of committee that should usually be assigned the special or temporary status is a building committee. This type of committee usually completes its work when a building is completed and accepted by the church.

The best approach to take is to assign a committee its status when it is formed. This answers in the beginning the question of what will happen to the committee.

Criteria

What criteria should a church use to determine which committees are needed? Suggestions provided here are not intended to be exhaustive, but they can help a church evaluate its committee structure.

Administrative needs—The basic question a church needs to ask is, What administrative need exists that would require a committee? Some needs relate more to ministry responsibilities than church administrative tasks. For example, if a need exists to take a census, this need should be assigned to the ministry organization responsible for outreach. In most cases this would be the Sunday School.

Another example could be assigning the Lord's Supper responsibilities to the deacons. This responsibility relates to the deacons' role in proclaiming the gospel.

Examples of administrative needs include maintaining facilities, administering the financial program, allocating and distributing volunteer leaders, and determining the public relations and publicity program of the church. Many more administrative needs exist in churches depending on size, location, age, and so forth. Each church should determine whether the needs are administrative or ministry related.

Clearly defined duties—A good test of determining if a committee is needed is whether the duties can be clearly written. If writing the exact duties of a committee is difficult, perhaps the committee is not needed. One thing should be clear: Do not begin a committee until the duties are clearly written. Suggested committee duties are presented in chapters 4 and 5.

Available resources—All committees need resources. Money is a resource needed by many committees. People and time are other resources that must be considered. If a church is unwilling to designate money, time, and personnel to a committee, questions should be asked about the need for beginning a new committee or continuing a present committee.

Relationships

Many problems can be eliminated if relationships are clearly and carefully defined. How is a committee related to various individuals and groups in the church? Several possibilities will be suggested in some cases. Each church should determine, prayerfully and carefully, what exact relationships are necessary for committees to function properly.

Pastor and staff—The pastor and staff members must be involved in committee work. They do not necessarily have to attend all committee meetings, but they must know what committees are doing or planning. In most cases, they are not regular members of committees. Some churches designate the pastor and staff members as advisors to various committees. As advisors, they help the committees solve problems, schedule meetings, and complete job assignments.

In some churches, the pastor or a staff member may be assigned to coordinate committees.

That person would provide training and orientation for all committees, assist in planning their budgets, and work with them to see that they function properly.

Committee chairpersons should notify the pastor or appropriate staff member when the committee is planning to meet. If a potential conflict exists, the pastor or staff member will be able to help the chairperson.

Ex officio—Another relationship is *ex officio* which means "by virtue of office or position." A church's bylaws should explain when, how, and why a person may serve as *ex officio*. Usually if there is no written document stating the specifics of *ex officio* members, the strongest person or tradition wins out.

Church Leadership Team (formerly Church Council)—In some churches committee chairpersons serve on the Church Leadership Team as regular members. In others the committee chairpersons attend Church Leadership Team meetings as necessary. The relationship of committees to the Church Leadership Team must be spelled out clearly to all committees.

Deacons—This is an area that causes much discussion and concern in church life. How do committees relate to deacons? Should all committees be required to report to the deacons before presenting a recommendation to the church? Should a deacon serve on every committee? Should a deacon serve as chairperson of every committee?

These and other questions have to be answered as a committee develops its committee structure. The answers are not simple. A church's history and current practice may dictate answers to some of these questions. Some churches and deacon groups are not willing to change easily. Church leaders need to be practical in trying to make changes in long-standing practices.

Robert Sheffield made the following statements concerning the relationship of deacons to committees: "Church committees receive direction from and report to the congregation on their work. They do not bring their reports to the deacons for approval before reporting to the congregation. Church committees, however, should keep the deacons informed about critical matters which affect the welfare of the congregation and the mission of the church."[1]

Other committees and ministry teams (councils)—When a committee's work relates to other committees, it should keep those committees informed. When its work relates to a ministry organization, the committee should keep that organization's ministry team informed.

Congregation—A committee is responsible to the congregation if that committee has been established as a church committee to perform administrative work for the congregation. This means that periodic reports should be made to the congregation concerning the work that has been assigned to the committee. These reports can be written or verbal, but they should be made. The frequency of the reports should be established when the committee is formed.

Steps for Establishing Committee Structure

Most churches already have committees. However, most churches need to study their committee structure to make it more effective. The steps offered are suggestions only. Each church should modify them according to its situation.

Assign the job. The beginning point involves assigning some group the responsibility for studying the church's committee structure and bringing recommendations to the congregation. This can be accomplished in several ways. One way is to elect a special committee with the assignment of (1) determining the criteria for church committees, (2) analyzing the present committee structure, and (3) recommending to the congregation needed changes in committee structure, including revised committee job descriptions.

Another possibility would be to assign this responsibility to the Church Leadership Team. A third choice is to ask the deacons to take this responsibility. In some cases, if the church has the staff available, the staff will be asked to make suggestions and help the committee or group that has been assigned the responsibility.

Select the criteria. Once a group has the responsibility for the study, the group must determine the criteria to be used in setting up committees. These criteria have already been discussed in an earlier section of this chapter. The committee or group should consider the criteria suggested or write new criteria.

Analyze present committees. The next step in the process calls for the group or committee to analyze present committees. Analysis should include the following actions:

1. Examine the present committee job descriptions to see whether updating is necessary.
2. Determine whether certain committees are still needed.
3. Determine whether any present committee assignments can be given to existing ministry organizations or groups.
4. Determine whether all needs being assigned to committees are administrative in nature.
5. Determine whether relationships are spelled out appropriately.
6. Survey all committee job descriptions to check for overlapping or duplicating assignments.
7. Determine whether necessary resources are available for the committees to function.
8. Analyze the number of committee members needed for each committee.

Recommend needed changes. The final step in the process involves recommending needed changes to the congregation. The needed changes usually fall under several categories.

1. *New committees*—As a result of analyzing the present committee structure and the administrative needs discovered through the survey, new committees may be needed. If new committees are needed, the group should clearly define the duties, establish relationships, and determine the number of committee members.
2. *Elimination/combination of committees*—Often after an analysis, committees can be eliminated. The needs for which they were originally established may no longer exist. In some cases, the committee duties can be combined with duties of other committees.
3. *Revision of committee job descriptions*—As a result of the study and analysis, job descriptions of committees often need to be rewritten.
4. *Reassigned work*—Often the study will show that some work can be assigned to an

existing organization. For example, the deacons may take the responsibility for the Lord's Supper. One church which studied its committee structure made the following changes:

- Committees were reduced in number from 24 to 19. The study committee discovered, for example, that a kindergarten committee still existed when the church had disbanded its kindergarten program three years before the study was conducted.
- All committee job descriptions were revised.
- Staff advisors were named to every committee.
- The rotation system was put into effect.
- The trustee committee was removed from the committee list because trustees are considered church officers.
- The number of committee members required for each committee was established. In previous years, no consistency existed in the number of committee members required.
- The music committee was disbanded. The responsibility for the music planning, coordination, and evaluation was assigned to a newly formed music ministry team.

A church needs to analyze its committee structure from time to time. Committee job descriptions, policies, and procedures should never become static instruments. They should be updated every year as committees are elected and needs change.

Determining a church's committee structure can be a painful process, but it can also be an enlightening and helpful experience for a church.

---

[1]Robert Sheffield, *The Ministry of Baptist Deacons* (Nashville: Convention Press, 1990), 33.

Resource

Michael D. Miller, *Church Leadership Team Handbook.* Nashville: Convention Press, 1995.

Chapter 3

DUTIES OF
CHURCH OFFICERS

A church's constitution and bylaws should establish the duties of church officers and should provide guidelines by which each church officer must act. Church officers must be careful to act only within the authority described for them by the church. Abiding by the guidelines provided in the constitution and bylaws can prevent potential problems.

Baptist churches traditionally have the following officers: moderator, clerk, treasurer, and trustees. The moderator, clerk, and treasurer are positions that require only one person to serve in that capacity. However, three trustees are usually elected.

Moderator

Who should serve as moderator? Many churches ask their pastors to serve as moderator. However, in other churches, the chairperson of deacons is moderator of the church. Other churches elect a moderator from the congregation for a one- to three-year term. The moderator is supposed to maintain the fellowship of the church. The role of the moderator is to facilitate the work of the church through the most harmonious route.

What is a moderator? The dictionary defines a moderator as a presiding officer. *Robert's Rules of Order* makes a chairperson synonymous with moderator and defines this person as the presiding officer.[1] A moderator has at least six functions.

1. *Maintain the fellowship.*
2. *Conduct orderly church business.*
3. *Execute church business in a timely manner.*
4. *Clarify church business for later action.*
5. *Keep on course with the business meeting agenda.*
6. *Speak for the church in times of crises.*

The moderator should work with other key leaders and church staff to develop an agenda for the business meeting. This agenda should then be published for church members to have appropriate information before the meeting. An agenda enables members to become more involved in the church's business life.

To facilitate the orderly conduct of church business, the duties of the moderator should be understood by both the moderator and the church.

Church Clerk

Because there is a great potential for litigation against churches, a church needs to maintain thorough and complete records of its business. Following are duties of church clerks:

1. *Record minutes.* When keeping minutes, the church clerk should:
   - Record the motions with the exact wording. The church clerk should request that those making motions put them in writing. If this is not possible, the clerk should repeat the motion as it is being recorded before the motion is seconded or voted on.
   - Record only necessary items of discussion. No attempt should be made to include every statement presented in discussion.
   - Always get the name of the person making the motion and seconding it. Should future questions arise concerning the intent or wording of a motion, knowing who made the motion can help clarify any questions.
   - Not editorialize in the minutes—that is, give an opinion concerning the motion or discussion. The church clerk records only the actual motion, the actual transaction of business, or what the moderator instructs. This procedure is important because these minutes become the legal documents supporting the action of the church.

2. *Preserve records.* The church clerk is responsible for preserving records. How much actual work the clerk does depends on how much the church staff helps with records. In some churches a staff secretary is responsible for maintaining membership records, and the records of business transactions are maintained by the church clerk.

Preserving records is a serious matter. Having a thorough record of the church's business has been the best protection against injurious law suits. Well-kept records can also provide orientation for new staff and church leaders.

3. *Correspond with other churches for membership changes.* In some churches the clerk is responsible for requesting and forwarding letters of membership to other churches. In churches with paid secretaries, this work may be assigned to them.

4. *Provide records for church history.* The clerk should work with the history committee to ensure they have the proper information for historical purposes. The following items should be kept for historical purposes: budgets; outstanding events; a record of new staff members; and a record of special events, such as remodeling, anniversaries, and celebration of centennials.

5. *Prepare the Annual Church Profile.* The church clerk is responsible for preparing the Annual Church Profile and sending it to the association. Some churches make this assignment to a church secretary. The Annual Church Profile is another important document and requires intentional effort by the church clerk.

Church Treasurer

The work of the church treasurer is focused on three financial categories: receiving, accounting, and dispersing monies. The treasurer's involvement depends on the church size, the number of staff, and other key leader involvement. One of the most important issues for the church treasurer is to protect the church's money and those involved in handling the church's money. The church should establish policies and procedures that require the church's money to pass through several hands. For more information about policies and procedures related to processing a church's monies, see *Managing Your Church Finances . . . Made Easy*, by J. David Carter.

The following are duties or functions of a church treasurer.

1. Counsel with the stewardship committee. The treasurer should counsel with the stewardship committee to develop and recommend policies and procedures related to receiving, accounting, and dispersing church monies. If the stewardship committee does not have this responsibility, the treasurer should work with the appropriate committee to develop these policies.

2. Maintain records of funds received and dispersed. An adequate procedure and record of receipts and disbursements should be kept. The treasurer should work with the stewardship committee in enlisting laypersons to receive, count, and deposit the money. After the money is deposited, the deposit slip should be verified. The treasurer or financial secretary should justify the financial records monthly.

3. Maintain records of contributions. The treasurer should work with the financial secretary to record member's contributions. This record serves as the financial statement of members' contributions. In some churches, the treasurer's responsibility with member's contribution records is limited because some churches have a part-time or full-time secretary responsible for this function.

4. Sign checks in accordance with church policies and procedures. The church treasurer should sign checks according to church policies and procedures. Supporting data should be presented when a check is requested. Most churches require cosigners on checks to protect the church's money and the people involved.

5. Make reports to appropriate committees and to the church. Depending on how a church is organized, the treasurer should make reports to the stewardship committee or finance committee. Then a subsequent report should be made to the church.

Trustees

What is a trustee? A paper written by Porter W. Routh states: "The office of a trustee is called into being by the relationship of the church to the state rather than by any scriptural injunction. The courts have held that it is impossible for a volunteer society (therefore a church) to sue or be sued, and therefore it cannot hold legal title. Unless a church is incorporated, it is necessary that the legal titles be conveyed to trustees who hold the property in trust for the society as beneficiary."[2]

Laws differ from state to state concerning incorporation. Each church should check with its secretary of state regarding the correct procedure for incorporating. Generally, the application must give correct information such as the name, the denomination with which your group plans to affiliate, the purpose of the organization, the location of the church, and a list of trustees. This application must be signed by those making the petition and must be notarized.

Because trustees should act only at the discretion and direction of the church, they are considered as church officers rather than a committee. Trustees serve as legal representatives in all transactions of the church. They hold legal title to the church property and sign all documents related to the purchase, sale, mortgaging, or rental of church property after approval by the church in regular business session.

In some cases churches elect trustees on the same basis as committees, using the rotation system. In other churches, trustees are elected permanently unless they move away, die, or resign. The following are duties of trustees:

1. ***Act as legal agents as directed by the church.*** Trustees can never act independently of the church. If a trustee acts without the authority of the church, he is personally responsible for the actions. Porter Routh, in the article, "What Is a Trustee?" said: "That a trustee cannot act on his own initiative or on his own behalf should be clearly understood. A trustee is selected by vote of confidence of the body which selects him, and the law demands perfect good faith and integrity of the trustee in the discharge of his obligation."[3]

Churches must spell out exactly how trustees should function, and trustees must clearly understand their function and act according to the prescribed content of the documents with which the church is incorporated.

2. ***Maintain inventory of all legal documents.*** Legal documents include mortgage loans, property deeds, and insurance. These documents are usually kept in a safe deposit box with copies filed in the church office. Some churches have an insurance committee charged with the responsibility of keeping the insurance program up-to-date. In this case the trustees should be informed of the coverage provided through the insurance program.

3. ***Counsel with other committees or organizations concerning legal matters.*** Often trustees can provide counsel to the property and space committee, stewardship committee, insurance committee, and deacons. Trustees can inform these groups concerning legal matters only. However, trustees have no authority for making decision without the church's action.

---

[1] Darwin Patnode, *Robert's Rules of Order: The Modern Edition* (New York: Berkley Books, 1989), 110.
[2] Porter Routh, "What Is a Trustee?" (Church Administration Department, Sunday School Board of the Southern Baptist Convention, 1969-70).
[3] Ibid.

Resources

Donna Gandy, *Ministry Office Quicksource: Guide to Essential Office Functions.* Nashville: LifeWay Press, 1998.
J. David Carter. *Managing Your Church's Finances . . . Made Easy.* Nashville: LifeWay Press, 1998.

Chapter 4

DUTIES OF PERMANENT COMMITTEES

A permanent committee is one that is called into being by the bylaws of the church and is sustained until removed from the bylaws by the church. The following are recommended as permanent committees.

Church Baptism Committee

In many churches the deacons have responsibility for the ordinances of baptism and the Lord's Supper. In some churches, the two committees whose work relates to the ordinances are designated deacon committees; in others they are called church committees. These duties apply to whoever has responsibility for this work.

The primary purpose of the baptism committee is to assist the pastor in preparing for and administering baptism. Duties of the baptism committee include:

1. *See that all necessary baptismal equipment and facilities are available and ready prior to each baptismal service.* This committee should see that the baptismal pool is ready, all robes and towels are ready, and everything is in order for the baptismal service.

2. *Recommend to the property and space committee additional or different equipment and space as needed.* At budget planning time the baptism committee should make in writing its request for equipment and supplies to the budget planning committee. This would include baptismal robes, towels, hair dryers, handkerchiefs, and other supplies needed in the baptismal area.

3. *Notify candidates for baptism well in advance of the scheduled baptism and provide the pastor with a list of those who will be present.* In some churches this responsibility is assigned to a church secretary. If the baptism committee has this responsibility, it should keep the pastor informed about the times needed for baptism and also communicate with the persons charged with the responsibility of filling the baptistry.

4. *Arrange with the pastor and candidates for a period of instruction.* Often the pastor has a set time before each baptismal service for this period of instruction. This must be worked out in cooperation with the pastor. The committee can assist in getting the candidates together for this instruction.

5. *Prepare names on flash cards for identification purposes.* When several persons are being baptized, the committee should prepare flash cards with the names of the baptismal candidates for the pastor. The card can be pinned at eye-level to the shoulder of the candidate's robe. This procedure helps the pastor call each person's name properly and eliminates any chance of embarrassment for the pastor or the candidate.

6. *Keep an official record of baptisms.* The baptism committee should keep accurate records about persons who are baptized. The name of each person baptized should be given to the church clerk or appropriate church secretary as soon after the baptismal service as possible. This will allow the clerk or secretary to keep the church membership records accurate and up-to-date.

7. *Assist at baptism times.* The baptism committee members should meet the candidates for baptism at the appointed time. The committee members should show candidates the dressing room, answer questions that may arise, and assist them in dressing and getting the towels and handkerchiefs ready.

8. *Assist the pastor at baptismal time.* Assisting the pastor at this point will include helping place the persons in the proper order for baptism, checking the pool for proper water level and temperature, and seeing that the lighting is handled properly in the pool and auditorium. Committee members should also see that the sound system is ready if it is used in the baptismal area.

Committee members should help the candidates enter and leave the pool and to the dressing room. One committee member should assist the pastor in getting dressed for the baptismal service. The committee members should be available to help the baptismal candidates until they are completely dressed and are ready to leave for the worship service. The committee members should prepare the baptismal area for the next baptismal service. Robes, towels, and handkerchiefs should be prepared for delivery to the laundry.

Church Benevolence Committee

The benevolence committee is primarily responsible for studying the needs of church families and other people in the community to whom the church ministers. They also need to formulate a plan for meeting those needs.

Following are duties for the benevolence committee:

1. *The benevolence committee should establish the amount of and frequency of assistance to be provided by the church to individuals or families.*

2. *The committee should locate church members and community persons who can provide appropriate assistance.* The committee can use surveys, conduct interviews, ask for help from church members, and consult other resource persons in the community to discover needs.

3. *Work with other groups in the church that provide benevolent actions.* These groups may include Sunday School, Woman's Missionary Union, or deacon family ministry groups. The benevolence committee may serve as a coordinating group for all these groups.

4. *Survey and determine available community agencies.* Many communities have agencies that provide assistance. Sometimes a church cannot provide the kind of help people need but can refer them to appropriate agencies. This committee should have a list which includes the type of services available, the address, the phone number, and contact persons for each community resource.

5. *Recommend budget requests for monies needed for ministering to people.* At budget planning time the committee should make its request to the church for monies. In some churches benevolence money comes from love offerings.

6. *Investigate and administer benevolence resources as needed.* When requests come to the church for help and are referred to the benevolence committee, the committee should investigate and administer resources as necessary. In most cases the policy should be observed that no money is given directly to persons in need. Money may be used to pay utilities, buy groceries, and so forth; it should seldom be given directly to individuals.

7. *Make reports to the church.* Periodically the benevolence committee should report the type of services provided, results of the benevolence work, and the amount of expenditures. A record should be kept of services provided. One church uses a card to record the name and social security number of each person to whom assistance is provided along with the type and amount of assistance.

Church Committee on Committees

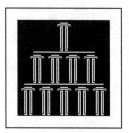

The purpose of the committee on committees is to select, enlist, and nominate persons to serve on church committees. The committee on committees helps reduce the large work load of the nominating committee. Some of the functions of the committee on committees are listed below:

1. *Review committee policies and procedures and make recommendations to the church.* Policies for committee work are discussed in chapter 9. This committee would have responsibility for recommending changes, additions, or deletions in the number and kind of committees.

2. *Review committee duties and make recommendations for revisions to the church.* Generally, committee duties do not change from year to year. But often new committees are added, some are combined with other committees, and some are deleted. The committee on committees should have responsibility for studying and recommending these changes annually to the church.

3. *Select, enlist, and nominate members and present them to the church for approval.* The committee on committees should adopt and facilitate a process for securing committee chairpersons each year to fill vacancies at the beginning of the church year. The committee should also adopt a process for filling any vacancies that occur during the year. Churches that

use the rotation system would have to fill only one third of the positions annually. The nomination of the committee members should take place in time for committee members to be oriented and trained for the new church year or whenever they take office.

Church Flower Committee

The flower committee provides a needed service in most churches. The worship area in a church is enhanced by the presence of flowers. The recommended duties of the flower committee are listed below:

1. *Suggest and recommend procedures for securing, arranging, and disposing of flowers for church services.* Definite policies should be determined to guide members in requesting an opportunity to place memorial flowers in the sanctuary. The committee should see that proper recognition is given to the memorial flowers. Suggested questions for determining guidelines for providing flowers follow:

- For which service will the church have flowers?
- How much shall be budgeted for flower arrangements?
- Who will provide the flowers?
- What arrangements will be made for memorial flowers?
- Will the flowers be used for more than one service?
- Will artificial flowers be used and to what extent?

2. *Formulate the recommended policies related to providing flowers for sick and bereaved members.* The following questions will help in formulating policies:

- To whom will flowers be sent? Members? Family members of church members? Others?
- How serious must an illness be before flowers are sent on behalf of the church?
- What price range will be used in purchasing flowers for sick and bereaved members?

3. *Work with the budget committee in requesting flower committee budget.* The flower committee should determine whether any artificial flower arrangements, vases, or flower stands need to be replaced. If so, budget recommendations should be submitted to the budget planning committee.

4. *Secure and provide flower arrangements for church services and for the sick and bereaved.* After policies have been determined, the flower committee should implement these policies by providing flowers for the services and for the sick and bereaved. In no case should the committee vary from the established policies.

5. *Dispose of flower arrangements.* The flower committee should be responsible for disposing of flowers. Wilted arrangements should not be left in the worship area. The flower committee should see to the timely disposal of all flowers. If a policy does not exist regarding the method of disposing of good arrangements, the committee should establish one. Many churches distribute these arrangements to shut-ins or hospitalized members.

Church Food Service Committee

Food service supports a church's busy schedule. Food service may vary from a formal food service to covered-dish meals. Other aspects of food service may include luncheons, fellowships, and wedding preparations. The following duties suggest some of the food service committee's responsibilities.

1. Determine the food service needs of the church. The committee should consult with staff and church leaders to determine food service needs.

2. Recommend food services to be provided. Once the needs are determined, the committee should recommend to the church the appropriate food services. These recommendations should be discussed and adopted by the church.

3. Recommend to the personnel committee the needed personnel for the food service program. The personnel committee has responsibility for employing persons in this area. The food service committee should suggest to the personnel committee the types of persons needed, the duties, and other qualifications.

4. Recommend to the budget planning committee the money needed for food services. The food service committee should forecast the budget needs for food services and should present the budget to the budget planning committee or stewardship committee at the appropriate time.

5. Develop and recommend policies and procedures related to food services. Policies needed include the types of services provided, the cost, scheduling procedures, and all matters related to the food service committee. These policies should be studied and developed by the food service committee. After the committee has settled on policies, the policies should be recommended to the church for adoption.

Church History Committee

The church history committee is responsible for keeping an up-to-date history of the church. Some of their duties are listed.

1. Gather and preserve historical records. A history committee needs to preserve many records. Legal documents include minutes, reports of church organizations, membership rolls, bulletins, pictures, proceedings, special correspondence, newspaper clippings, periodical clippings, biographical materials, and association/convention records. These all should be preserved by the history committee. The history committee should determine a document retention system.

2. Set up and maintain a storage system for all historical records. Some churches have special areas for storage. Other churches have a special heritage or historical room where such information is stored. The history committee should set up procedures for storing these |valuable pieces of information.

3. *Plan and implement special projects as needed.* Often in a church's life, special occasions arise that are of historical value. Such occasions may include anniversaries, building dedications, and centennial celebrations. The history committee can plan and implement these occasions as special projects.

A church's history committee should plan and develop a book about its history. A writer for the church's history could come from within the church, or someone who is not a church member could be commissioned to write the book. This project would require many months of planning, writing, and significant investigation by the author. Though some churches are young, preserving records from the earliest times is wise.

Church Lord's Supper Committee

In many churches the deacons have the responsibility for conducting the Lord's Supper. However, some churches assign the responsibility of the Lord's Supper to a committee. Following are some of their functions:

1. *Have all necessary Lord's Supper equipment and materials in place prior to each observance of the ordinance.*

2 *Assist in planning and evaluating the observance of the Lord's Supper.* This committee could help the pastor and deacons develop the plan and schedule the dates for the ordinance to be conducted throughout the year.

3. *Arrange for all Lord's Supper equipment to be gathered, cleaned, and stored after the observance.*

4. *Maintain an inventory of equipment and recommend purchase of additional equipment as needed.*

Church Nominating Committee

The nominating committee's principle function is to lead in staffing all church-elected leadership positions filled by volunteers. Suggested duties are as follows:

1. *Select, interview, and enlist church ministry organization leaders, other church leaders, and general officers.* The church ministry organization leaders consist of Sunday School director, Discipleship Training director, Baptist Men On Mission director, Woman's Missionary Union director, and church music director (if that position is filled by a volunteer). Other church leaders include the director of the church library ministry and the director of the recreation ministry. General church officers are moderator, clerk, treasurer, and trustees.

In some churches, staff members are assigned the responsibility for enlisting some ministry organization leaders. For example, the minister of education may be responsible for enlisting the Sunday School director and Discipleship Training director. This should be coordinated through the nominating committee.

2. *Screen volunteers before they are invited to serve.* If screening is done, it should be done before the enlistment process. Potential candidates may be asked these questions: Are you able and willing to serve? Is there anything that would prevent you from serving? An important outcome of these two questions is that every qualified person has the opportunity to say yes or no about serving. Allowing each person the opportunity to respond to the possibility of serving in the kingdom is important.

3. *Distribute volunteer leaders according to priority needs.* A church has only so many leaders. Priorities often dictate where leaders should be used. Leaders should be placed where their talents can best be used to help a church be what God would have it be.

4. *Assist in discovering and enlisting persons to fill leadership positions.* The nominating committee should serve as a resource for ministry or organization leaders in discovering potential workers. The nominating committee could conduct talent surveys, distribute questionnaires, and conduct interviews with prospective volunteer leaders to discover talents.

5. *Present volunteer leaders to the church.* After the enlistment process, the nominating committee is responsible for presenting all leaders to the church for election. Electing volunteer leaders by church vote magnifies the positions, places a greater responsibility on those who accept positions, and communicates to the church the significance of serving in God's kingdom.

Church Personnel Committee

The primary purpose of the personnel committee is personnel administration. The personnel committee should be an advocate for the church staff, including the pastor and other staff, to protect the church's investment of time and money. The relationship of the personnel committee in supervising individual staff members should be clearly defined. Each employee should know who has the responsibility of employing and releasing personnel, who the supervisor is, and whom he or she may go to for help.

In some churches the personnel committee employs all staff members, such as the janitorial staff, secretarial staff, and pastoral leadership staff. In other churches the personnel committee is involved only in the pastoral leadership staff, such as the minister of music, minister of education, minister of youth, and so forth. In these churches a staff member, such as an administrator or minister of education, has responsibility for employing secretarial staff, janitorial staff, and food service personnel.

Recommended duties of the personnel committee are listed below.

1. *Study and recommend the need for additional church staff positions.* The personnel committee should be forward-looking and should recognize the need for additional staff members and make appropriate recommendations. The committee should rely on the pastor and other staff members in forecasting needs. Therefore, continuous communication should be maintained between staff members and personnel committee members and key leaders.

2. *Prepare and update job descriptions and organizational charts.* A job description helps clarify an individual's role on a church staff. Job descriptions serve as guidelines to help staff members stay involved and interested in their work.

The personnel committee should help write job descriptions for church staff members. Certain categories need to be included in job descriptions: the job title, principle function, responsibilities, and relationships. Since conditions change, responsibilities also change from time to time. The personnel committee should be aware of these changes and should be constantly in the process of updating job descriptions.

3. *Recruit, interview, and recommend new personnel.* Some personnel are recruited, interviewed, and recommended for employment by appropriate supervisors. But if the personnel committee has this responsibility, recruiting, interviewing, and recommending involves a great deal of time and effort.

Recruiting involves discovering potential workers and getting pertinent information concerning them. The interviewing process can take place on or off the church site. The next steps include recommending an appropriate job description to the church, sharing information about the person being considered, and recommending salary and other benefits.

4. *Develop and recommend a salary program for the church.* A complete salary program includes salary, expenses, and benefits. Included in the salary-benefits program should be privileges for staff members such as time away from duties for personal development, training, personal leave, and sabbatical.

5. *Develop and recommend policies and procedures for staff members.* Staff members deserve to know what is expected of them and what allowances are provided. The personnel committee should develop a manual or booklet that includes policies and procedures related to all church staff. This policies and procedures manual should include such things as absences, employment practices, leaves, salary administration, vacation, time off, working hours, and dress code. The committee should spell out specifics in these areas to lessen confusion. Answering questions in advance saves time and prevents misunderstanding.

Church Preschool/Children's Ministry Committee

The purpose of the preschool/children's ministry committee is to coordinate all activities and ministries of the various church organizations as they relate to preschoolers and children. Preschool and children's church ministry organizations and teachers use similar teaching methods and share the same rooms and furnishings. Accomplishing a quality ministry for preschoolers and children requires coordinated planning among their leaders, parents, and other church leaders. The preschool/children's ministry committee should include representatives from Sunday School, Discipleship Training, Music Ministry, Woman's Missionary Union, and weekday education. Additional members may include the preschool/children's coordinator, preschool and children's division directors, a father and a mother of preschoolers/children (not from the same family), director of the ministry to expectant and new parents, the directors of day care

and/or kindergarten programs, and the chairperson of the weekday education committee. If possible, include people with expertise in early childhood education or child development, legal issues, social work, business and finance, and medicine.

Duties of the preschool committee include the following:

1. *Recommend and publicize preschool policies and procedures.*
2. *Recommend the purchase of furnishings and supplies.*
3. *Coordinate space assigned to preschool work.*
4. *Select, train, and supervise employed preschool teachers.*
5. *Communicate regularly with the Church Leadership Team.*

Church Property and Space Committee

The purpose of the church property and space committee is to assist the church in caring for all property and buildings. The duties of the committee follow.

1. **Inspect all church properties periodically.** Depending on the size of the church properties, the committee should make inspections periodically. An inventory of all property should be maintained. The purpose of inspecting and inventory is to plan for preventive maintenance work.

2. **Consult with ministry leaders concerning space allocations.** From year to year, space allocations change for ministry organizations. Some adjustments may need to be made. The property and space committee should work with ministry leaders to ensure everyone has needed space.

3. **Recommend changes in the use of facilities and property.** Often changes must be made for the use of space. For example, an adult department may need to move to another area. The choir room may need to be moved because of a lack of space. The committee should work with the organizations and groups involved to make the best recommendations for everyone.

4. **Make recommendations concerning employment, training, and supervision of maintenance personnel.** These recommendations should be made to the personnel committee. One person should supervise maintenance personnel. The property and space committee can make recommendations to the supervisor about maintenance personnel.

5. **Develop and recommend policies and procedures related to church property and space.** The recommended policies and procedures should include maintenance, insurance, and use of buildings, property, and space. Some churches have a separate insurance committee to handle the insurance recommendations. Policies and procedures should be developed by this committee, published for church members, and adopted by the church. After adopting the policies and procedures, each organization and service group should receive a copy. The policies and procedures should be reviewed periodically with leaders; they also should be published and distributed to church members for review.

6. Develop and recommend arranging, equipping, and supervising parking space.
Church parking is a problem with many churches. The property and space committee should continually evaluate the parking needs. This committee should also be looking for new space that might be available for parking.

7. Prepare budget recommendations. At budget time each year the property and space committee should plan its work and provide these details for the new year's budget. Budget recommendations should be made to the budget planning committee or the stewardship committee.

8. Consult with church organization leaders and other groups concerning furnishings.

Church Public Relations Committee

The purpose of the church public relations committee is communication. The scope of this communication is the church's work. The target group for this communication is church members and the community. Duties of the committee include the following:

1. Determine the understanding and acceptance of the church's identity. A church must have a good idea of what its identity is before attempting to communicate it. Determining and understanding this identity is the beginning point for developing a positive image within the community facilitated by public relations. To establish a new identity a church must discover community and church needs, plan strategies for meeting those needs, prioritize present resources, and continually evaluate plans or strategies.

2. Work with church leaders to communicate to their audience. Church leaders, such as pastoral ministry leaders and ministry organization leaders, have a responsibility to communicate through various media to their target audiences. The public relations committee should assist these leaders in their tasks.

3. Help church members become aware of the value of good church public relations. Often church members do not see the value of effective church public relations because they do not understand what public relations means. Every church has a public relations image—anywhere from poor to excellent. Therefore, the public relations committee can help change that image if it needs to be changed.

4. Develop and recommend policies and procedures to improve the church's public relations work. Policies and procedures are needed in the area of public relations. These policies include who will be the church's spokesperson in times of crises and who will be responsible for developing news items and stories.

5. Develop and recommend policies for the purpose, content, and updating of the church's Web site and electronic signs, if the church communicates by these means.

Church Stewardship Committee

The purpose of the church stewardship committee is to develop a program that includes budget development, budget subscription, and budget administration along with stewardship development.

The duties of the committee are as follows:

1. Develop the budget. The stewardship committee has responsibility for developing the church's budget. Once a church has established its annual program of work, a budget can be planned and adopted to implement this program. In budget development, several important areas of work need to be considered:

- recording giving and potential giving of church members
- analyzing current strengths and weaknesses
- evaluating budget requests
- directing the annual budget preparation
- presenting the budget to the Church Leadership Team and the church for review
- presenting the budget to the church for adoption

2. Direct the subscription of the budget. Many churches use a budget subscription program after the budget has been adopted. The committee makes special plans for subscribing the funds to implement the budget. If a budget subscription process is being considered, several steps are recommended.

- Find and study the latest information on budget subscription.
- Share the results discovered on budget subscription with the pastor and appropriate groups.
- Recommend to the Church Leadership Team suggested dates for budget subscription.
- Conduct the campaign.
- Provide budget subscription information for public relations purposes.

3. Administer the budget. Once a budget has been planned, adopted, and subscribed, the committee is responsible for administering the budget. Sometimes this responsibility is given to a separate committee. Budget administration involves the following procedures:

- Approve budget expenditures.
- Compare expenditures with budget allocations.
- Recommend needed adjustments to the budget.
- Recommend adequate financial systems.
- Request an annual audit of financial records.

4. Promote stewardship education. A continuing program of stewardship education should be implemented in a church. The stewardship education program should include conducting special stewardship education projects, such as Christian money management and estate planning seminars. The stewardship education program should also keep church members informed regarding the Cooperative Program and associational mission support.

Church Weekday Education Committee

 The purpose of the weekday education committee is to coordinate all activities and ministries of various weekday programs and to serve as liaison between the weekday program and the church. The weekday education committee may be responsible for one or more kinds of weekday programs. Some of these programs include kindergarten, nursery school, preschool day care, mother's day out, school-age child care, Christian schools, day care for the handicapped, and senior adult day care.

Members of the weekday education committee are chosen through the nominating committee. Including persons who have expertise in the following areas is recommended: early childhood education or child development, legal matters, social work, business and finance, medical field, public relations, and personnel management. Parents of children in the program, deacons, senior adults, or representatives from other church ministry organizations also should be considered for committee membership. The duties of the weekday education committee are as follows:

1. *Determine policies and procedures for operating and administering the program.*
2. *Work in coordination with the personnel committee to staff the weekday education program.*
3. *Assist the program director in developing a workable budget.*
4. *Comply with all legal and licensing requirements.*
5. *Direct public relations efforts to inform, involve, and educate church members and community about the programs.*
6. *Coordinate the work of the program with other church activities involving young children.*
7. *Review reports and records to ensure proper operation of the program.*
8. *Report regularly to the church about the work of the weekday education program.*
9. *Organize the involvement of church members and parents as volunteers in the program.*

Churches may need other committees to implement their goals and priorities. These could include a prayer committee, a media ministry committee (radio, TV, Web site), a family ministry committee, or whatever a church's unique situation requires.

Chapter 5

DUTIES OF SPECIAL COMMITTEES AND MINISTRY TEAMS

Special committees are generally described as ad hoc or task force groups and have a specified time to function.

Church Building Steering Committee

The church building steering committee is a special committee. T. Lee Anderton in *The Church Property/Building Guidebook*[1] indicated that there are eight areas of work related to church building needs. They are

- Publicity
- Church growth
- Property
- Program
- Furnishings
- Finance
- Plans
- Construction

He recommended three options for committee structures depending on the size of the church and the size of the project.

- A large church or project committee is comprised of the steering committee with eight subcommittees.
- A smaller church or project can simplify the structure using the steering committee with four subcommittees.
- Small churches or small projects may need only a minimum organization and omit sub-committees completely.

For more information, see *Planning and Building Church Facilities*, by Gwenn E. McCormick.

The building steering committee has the following duties:

1. Gather, study, and analyze information about the church and the community. Establish an accurate picture of the church's future growth potential based on this study.

2. Study the property owned and the church's location in the community to determine the relationship of these factors to the church's ministry and growth potential.

3. Make recommendations concerning property needs.

4. *Design the space available to accommodate the church's ministries.*

5. *Determine what furnishings, and in consultation with music staff, what musical instruments are needed.* Persons involved in this step should consider items which may be memorial gifts.

6. *Survey the income potential of the church.*

7. *Conduct a fund-raising campaign.* Borrow funds needed and pay for work completed during the building program. Often the building finance subcommittee is a separate committee from the church stewardship (or finance) committee.

8. *See that the building is constructed according to specifications and is ready for use.*

Constitution and Bylaws Committee

The purpose of this committee is to prepare and recommend to the church a constitution and bylaws. The duties are listed below:

1. *Decide what should be included in the constitution and bylaws.* Request from your local secretary of state a copy of the model Nonprofit Corporation Act and use it as a guideline to determine the contents of your constitution and bylaws. If that is not available to you, include the following items in your constitution.

- preamble
- the name of the church (its official title)
- the objective of the church
- church doctrinal statement or articles of faith
- relationship of the church to other groups
- church covenant

Include these items in the bylaws:

- membership
- general church officers
- church committees
- ministry organizations
- ordinances
- church meetings
- church finances
- church operations manual amendments

2. *Compile the statements related to all areas of the constitution and bylaws.* This task can be done by assigning individuals or subcommittees to the various areas.

Whether assigned to individuals or subcommittees, the written proposal should be sent to all members of the committee. All committee members should have the opportunity to review and suggest changes in the proposed constitution and bylaws.

3. *Present the proposed constitution and bylaws to the church.* Church members should have plenty of time to study the report. Each section of the committee's report could be presented on different occasions, or the total constitution and bylaws could be presented with a complete

interpretation. Following interpretation, church members should have opportunity to study the report. After church members have had time to study the report, discussion should be held to answer all questions related to the report.

   4. Ask the church to adopt the constitution and bylaws. At the appropriate time the constitution and bylaws should be adopted by the church at a regular business meeting or at a specially called business meeting.

   5. Update the constitution and bylaws as necessary. A constitution and bylaws can become outdated. If a church spends the necessary time and energy to write and adopt a constitution and bylaws, it should be willing to maintain and keep the same document up-to-date. A special committee, the Church Leadership Team, or another appropriate group should periodically review the document. If revisions are necessary, they should be brought to the church for adoption.

Long-Range Planning Committee

The primary purpose of the long-range planning committee is to develop the church's priorities for several years. This period of time can be for one year, eighteen months, three years, or five years. Suggested duties are listed below:

   1. Discover the planning needs. To discover needs the committee must do a thorough analysis of the church and the community. Based on this analysis, the group will be able to pinpoint specific needs of the church—how the church will focus for the next several years. Relevant planning must be based on needs; therefore, this task represents a major step in the long-range planning process.

   2. Lead in setting church goals. Based on the needs discovered, the long-range planning committee should lead the church in setting long-range goals. Goals are statements of measurable results that the church expects to attain in a specific period of time—what does the church expect to accomplish and by when? Goals help a church pinpoint its targets for growth.

   3. Plan strategies for reaching the goals. Once the committee has established its target for growth, the next responsibility is to develop strategies for each of these goals. Strategies tell how the committee proposes to reach the goals. The strategies should contain one or more action plans. Action plans include projects, activities, meetings, and schedules. These action plans should be spread over a period of years. Each goal should have one strategy composed of one or more action plans.

   4. Complete the long-range plans. The committee has the responsibility for leading the church to adopt the plans. This process involves communicating to the church the goals, strategies, and action plans. The next step is to present the long-range plans to the congregation for discussion and voting. For the long-range plans to be accepted by the church, key leaders must be committed to them. To complete the plans, the committee should establish an evaluation and implementation process.

Pastor Search Committee

The primary purpose of the pastor search committee is to find and recommend someone to serve as pastor. This committee, naturally, should seek God's leadership through the Holy Spirit to direct them in this responsibility. For detailed information about the pastor search process, see *Pastor Search Committee Handbook.*

The following are suggested duties:

1. Establish guidelines for the work of the committee before it begins looking for a pastor. This committee must be in accord when it evaluates preaching, leadership, and personal ministry skills of prospective pastors. It must allocate time at the beginning of its work to understand theological concepts that guide it, to bond as a committee, and to understand the procedures for its work as outlined in the church's constitution and bylaws.

It must adopt a search process, develop communication guidelines for reporting to the church, prepare a committee budget, and develop a proposed pastor-church covenant of relationship. This covenant will outline what the church expects the pastor to do and what salary and benefits it will provide for him, including housing, insurance, ministry expenses, vacation, leave time, and retirement package. Then it should obtain authority from the church to negotiate based on the budget and covenant.

2. Develop a profile of what the church desires in a pastor. Collect information through written surveys or congregational meetings. What are its expectations in such areas as preaching, funerals, weddings, visitation, ministry to the sick and needy, special events, administration, evangelism, leadership, and being a visionary?

Develop profiles of your church and community for the prospective pastor to consider in return.

3. Gather prospect profiles. Prospect names may come from applications, recommendations, directors of missions, state convention offices, and seminary placement offices. Have each prospect fill out a standard biographical profile. Consider types of experiences in ministry, the average tenure in each position, education, family background, and interests.

4. Choose five top prospects. Request audio or video tapes of two recent sermons from each. Inform all other applicants that you are not considering them at this time, and thank them for applying.

5. Focus on one prospect. Check references and interview him and his wife in a neutral location. What is the candidate's attitude about church members, staff members, volunteer leaders, the denomination, worship design, missions education, and stewardship? What are the person's qualifications as a preacher? The committee should consider the candidate's call, knowledge of the Bible, ability to communicate, and feelings about the Bible's place in preaching.

If the committee wishes to proceed further with this prospect, it should go hear him preach, interview him and his wife again, and negotiate details of what the committee would recommend to the church. At this time the committee should decide whether to continue with this person.

6. Recommend a pastor to the church. When the committee has agreed on a prospective pastor, it should provide the church with information about him and his wife. Invite them to meet the church, and have the church hear him preach at morning worship. Recommend him to the church, and then vote as a church. Encourage a unanimous vote. Inform the pastor of the vote, and inform the church of his response.

7. Plan welcoming activities and an installation service for the pastor and his family. Notify the association and state convention that your church has a new pastor.

Church Ushers Committee

Church ushers are committee members in some churches and officers in other churches. Ushers perform a unique ministry. Their duties are considered below.

1. Greet people before and after worship services. Many people coming to church will have personal contact only with an usher. The kind of impression the usher makes often influences the visitor's attitude about the church. Ushers should be in their places at least 15 minutes before the worship service begins. They should greet and make persons feel welcome as they enter the worship area. Ushers should try to learn people's names so they may call them by name as they are welcomed to the services. A warm welcome will help create the right atmosphere for worship.

2. Seat people during the service. Many people tend to sit in the same place. Ushers should learn where people like to sit. Prompt seating of people is an indication that ushers are aware of what is happening around them. Visitors should be seated beside regular attenders and introduced when possible. Other suggestions for seating people are
- seat people only at times when their entrance will not disturb the service;
- seat people near the front and center, if possible;
- walk slowly down the aisle;
- stop at the pew where the people are to be seated and form a gate into the pew by placing the hand on the back of the pew in front;
- give the church bulletin or other materials to the worshiper;
- be aware of places to seat people.

3. Provide information to people concerning the church. Ushers should be able to provide information about
- church facilities such as rest rooms, the church office, and telephones;
- schedules for Sunday School, worship services, and other ministries;
- first-aid equipment and necessary procedures in case of an emergency.

4. Distribute bulletins. Ushers have the primary task of distributing worship bulletins to everyone who enters the building. This will enable people to follow the order of service.

5. Receive the offerings. In most instances, ushers have responsibility for receiving the offering. They should be thoroughly oriented in proper procedures for this part of worship. Every usher should know his area of responsibility.

6. Be alert to needs of persons conducting the services. Ushers should be sensitive to the room temperature so people will be comfortable. If someone needs assistance, ushers should be ready and available to assist. People with special problems sometimes venture into an auditorium. When these kinds of emergencies develop, ushers should know specific procedures for dealing with the situation. Problems of this nature should be handled without involving the pastor or the staff.

7. *Help maintain order.*

Church Audio Services Committee

In some churches, volunteers maintain and operate a sophisticated sound system. Churches use different methods of having volunteers work in this area. In some churches this becomes a permanent committee, using a rotation system just as other committees do. However, in other churches a group of people who perform this task are considered a special group and do not fit into the category of church committees.

Only people with special knowledge and technical skills should operate a sound system. Therefore, using a rotation system for this committee is not recommended.

The following duties are suggested regardless of the structure used.

1. *Study and recommend the appropriate sound system.*

2. *Operate the sound system.* The sound system for worship areas and other places in the church will need expert operators. The audio services group should provide the operators as requested for special services and for regular services.

3. *Provide a maintenance program for upkeep of the equipment.* If someone in the audio services group does not have the expertise to maintain the equipment, a professional person or company should be employed to maintain the equipment. All electronic equipment needs periodic repair and maintenance. People who do not have the proper understanding of this equipment should not be allowed to work on the equipment; they perhaps could assist the specially hired or contracted group.

4. *Recommend changes in the audio system.* The audio services group should recommend changes in the sound system to update and make available the best possible sound system for the worship experience and other opportunities within the church.

5. *Make recommendations to the budget planning committee.*

MINISTRY TEAMS

A significant portion of committee work is now being coordinated through ministry teams (councils). A ministry team assists the ministry to determine its course, to coordinate ministry effort, and to relate to the Church Leadership Team for overall coordination. A church may have any or all of the following ministry teams: evangelism ministry team, missions development ministry team, student ministry ministry team, senior adult ministry team, single adult ministry team, and other age-group ministry teams.

Evangelism Ministry Team

The evangelism ministry team assists the church in several key ways:

- Interprets New Testament evangelism
- Plans and implements New Testament evangelism
- Properly relates how evangelism is conducted in the New Testament
- Assists the pastor and staff in leading the church to develop and implement an ongoing program of New Testament evangelism.
- Coordinates with the Church Leadership Team.

The evangelism ministry team is made up of three key persons who enlist others to serve with them. The three are the evangelism director, mass evangelism director, and personal evangelism director. The evangelism director serves on the Church Leadership Team. Members of the evangelism ministry team serve for a limited time during planning and implementing events.

The duties of the evangelism ministry team include the following:

1. *Develop and engage the church in a comprehensive plan of evangelism.*
2. *Involve church members in personal evangelism.*
3. *Plan and conduct special events of mass evangelism.*

On Mission Team

The On Mission Team leads the church to fulfill its missions responsibility.

The On Mission Team consists of a director and representatives from Woman's Missionary Union and Baptist Men On Mission. In larger-membership churches, members are added to direct projects; a missions survey director is also included. In church-type missions, the missions development director and missions survey director are the same person. The missions development director is a regular member of the Church Leadership Team.

The duties of the missions development ministry team are

- *identify mission needs and opportunities;*
- *develop mission strategies to respond to unmet needs;*
- *establish new churches;*
- *support establishment and strengthening of Woman's Missionary Union and Baptist Men on Mission.*

Age-group Ministry Teams

Coordination of age-group efforts may be accomplished in three ways: self-coordination, coordinating teams or committees, or age division coordination/directors. The approach used by a church is determined by the complexity of the organization within the age division. Self-coordination exists when organization leaders of an age division voluntarily coordinate their work and the use of space, equipment, and supplies.

Coordinating teams primarily serve in advisory and coordinating functions. Members of the teams represent preexisting organizational units of a particular age group. One from the group is elected by the group as a chairperson.

Several examples of age-group coordinating ministry teamss include youth, student, single adult, married adult, and senior adult. These ministry teams share basic responsibilities.

1. *Understand needs; develop, implement, and evaluate ministry to meet the needs.*
2. *Coordinate events and activities to protect the overall church schedule.*
3. *Coordinate space and supplies.*

Members consist of age-group organization representatives: Sunday School, Discipleship Training, Music Ministry, and missions—and in some cases parents and/or members-at-large.

Leaders are generally elected from within the group and serve as regular members of the Church Leadership Team.

A committee may be an age-group coordinating group—especially in the case of the preschool committee. Duties for this committee are covered in chapter 4.

---

[1]T. Lee Anderton, *The Church Property/Building Guidebook* (Nashville: Convention Press, 1980), 18-38.

Resources

Gwenn McCormick, *Planning and Building Church Facilities.* Nashville: Convention Press, 1992.

Pastor Search Committee Handbook. Nashville: LifeWay Press ®, 2002.

Chapter 6

COORDINATING CHURCH COMMITTEE WORK

*T*he *airplane pilot radioed the control tower and asked for permission to land. The control tower director, new on the job, said, "OK, please come in on the east end of runway 16."*

"Roger and out," replied the pilot.

Three seconds later, another pilot asked for permission to land. The new control tower director said: "OK, please come in on the west end of runway 16."

The captain replied hastily, "I just heard you tell the other captain to come in on the east end of runway 16."

"Yep," replied the control tower director, "that's right. Y'all be careful, you hear!"

Often coordination in committee work happens like this story. Chairpersons and committee members are enlisted, given a committee job description, and told: "Y'all go to it, but be careful, you hear!"

One dictionary definition of *coordinate* is "to harmonize in a common action." A synonym of *coordination* is *synchronizing*. *Synchronizing* means making things occur or happen at the same time or operating in unison.

Many committee activities need to be coordinated. Such things as when committees should meet, how committees work together on projects, when committees report to the church, and committee budgeting all require coordination. Churches cannot just give committees jobs to do and turn them loose. Someone or some organization needs to have the responsibility for coordination.

The following case study illustrates the need for coordinating committee work.

The church property and space committee had responsibility for planning the repair of the parking lot. The chairperson received bids from three companies. The other committee members were not informed of the steps being taken. The committee chairperson reported to the finance committee to request funds for repairs. The finance committee approved the request to be sent to the deacons and the church for a vote. (This was established procedure for nonbudget items.)

When the deacons received the report, they asked many questions, such as questions concerning the makeup of the fill for holes in the parking lot. The chairperson of the committee was absent from the deacons meeting, and several committee members who knew nothing about the project could not answer questions. This raised other questions in the minds of the deacons. As a result of the confusion, action was delayed on the proposed project.

This case study illustrates the need for every individual on the committee to be informed and all activities to be coordinated to achieve a common goal, which was, in this case, improving the parking lot.

Another case study illustrates the need for coordination among several committees and groups.

A stewardship committee meeting had been called for a Wednesday evening following prayer meeting to discuss several proposed projects. A planning and survey committee was scheduled for the same evening. The Church Leadership Team had also scheduled a meeting the same evening to discuss the fall schedule. A problem existed because several people were members of all three groups.

Another example of lack of coordination involved the public relations committee.

The finance committee asked a lawyer to study the contract the church had with a local TV station. The public relations committee was not consulted. This committee should have been the liaison between the church and the TV station.

Before anyone knew what was happening, the lawyers had approached the manager of the TV station. Fortunately, a staff member found out about this and was able to bring the public relations committee into the picture. Potential problems were averted.

What happens if a church does not have adequate coordination? As illustrated, it can have conflicts in meeting times. Duplication of work may occur when no one is responsible for coordinating committee work. Coordination must also take place at the committee level so all committee members know what is being done and when it is being done. Committee members need to be informed about all committee actions.

Areas for Coordination

Several areas of committee work need careful coordination.

Committee selection/election. Some group needs to be charged with the responsibility for selecting and electing committee members. Many churches have a policy that no person can serve on more than one standing or permanent committee. This requires a great deal of coordination during the selection and election process. (Committee selection and election are discussed in chapter 9.)

Committee organization. When a committee is established or committee work is being reorganized, someone or some group must have responsibility for coordinating the writing of job descriptions. This process will eliminate duplication of work.

Committee training. Just as ministry organization leaders are trained for their responsibilities, committee members need to be trained in how to fulfill their duties. A training program should be planned each year to help committee members understand their role and how they are to fulfill that role in the church. (Committee training is discussed in chapter 7.)

Projects/activities. When committees begin to function, working on projects and activities, they need to ensure that their work is concluded on time and that recommendations are made to the congregation at the proper time. Someone or some group that knows the procedures for making reports and recommendations—who must be notified and when—must be responsible for coordinating this process.

Reports. Reporting to the congregation or to appropriate groups requires that certain activities be conducted at specified times. If someone is not in a position to know when and how this action should occur, committees will often fail to perform their duties effectively, efficiently, and on time.

Budgeting. Many committees require monies from the budget to function appropriately. To have adequate funds for their activities, the request for budget monies should be made at the appropriate time. For this process to take place at the proper time and in the most effective way, coordination is necessary.

Groups/Entities Involved

A number of groups or entities need to be involved in the coordination process if committees are to be effective. A committee will not necessarily have to coordinate with each of these groups in its work, but committees should not overlook any of these groups in carrying out their responsibilities.

One of the groups involves other committees. Often a committee's work is related to other committee work in the church, as was the case in some of the illustrations cited earlier in this chapter. The committee chairperson should make sure he keeps other committees informed when the work of his committee involves other committees. Such would be the case when the committee has to go to the finance committee or appropriate group to ask for additional or new funds for a particular project.

In some churches, committee work is coordinated through the Church Leadership Team. Committee members may serve as regular or ex officio members of the Church Leadership Team. In these cases, all committee projects and activities would be coordinated by the Church Leadership Team.

Some churches require committees to report to the deacons. If this is the case in your church, much attention should be give to coordination at this level. Also, staff members need to be involved in the coordination process. Most of the committee work will affect some staff members. If so, the committee chairperson should make sure these staff persons are involved in the decision-making and implementing process.

Ultimately, the congregation will make the final decisions related to committee proposals in most churches. Obviously in these cases the congregation must be considered an entity to be involved in the coordination process.

Principles of Coordination

For coordination to be effective certain principles need to be considered. The following general principles may provide guidance for a church as it considers the coordination processes.

Coordination requires planning.—Coordination, to be effective, requires looking beyond the present. Schedules have to be considered. Work relationships have to be examined, and many other committee work assignments require taking a long look. The obvious result of not planning is confusion and a slowing down of the committee process.

Communication enhances coordination.—The importance of communication cannot be overemphasized. For coordination to be effective, adequate communication must be provided for all people, groups, and entities involved. The communication should be from staff to chairperson to members; it must also be from members to chairperson to staff to congregation.

Coordination requires harmonious objectives.—To win the game you must know the rules. You must know the goals to be reached. Assignments for reaching the goals (committee duties) should be understood by everyone. Each committee member should be involved in understanding the objectives of his or her committee.

Coordination involves cooperation.—Cooperation is a team effort. Consider some of the following, practical aspects of teamwork:

- Each committee member needs to understand the total problem or job to be done.
- Each committee member needs to see how she can contribute toward solving the problem or completing the work.
- Each committee member needs to be aware of the potential contribution of other individuals on the committee. This concept involves all team members recognizing that every other committee member is essential to the life of the team. Teamwork is basically a shared quest.
- Each team member needs to play a positive role in effecting the team's work.

Everyone must realize that teamwork involves give and take. Committee members must be willing to give themselves to the committee task, and they must also be willing to accept the ideas and contributions of other committee members.

Methods of Coordination

A church has many options in determining how to coordinate committee work. Smaller-membership churches usually have their committee work coordinated by the pastor. In some churches the committee work will be coordinated by the deacon chairperson. Some churches require the moderator to be responsible for committee coordination.

Larger-membership churches often use the staff-advisor approach to coordination. This method calls for staff members to be assigned to committees that relate to their area of work. For example, the business administrator would be assigned as staff advisor to such committees as the property and space committee, the food service committee, and the stewardship committee.

The minister of education would be assigned to committees such as public relations, history, and weekday education. The job of the staff advisor, when this method is used, could be as follows:

• Work with the chairperson to provide adequate training for committee members.
• Meet periodically with the committee chairperson to plan, coordinate, and evaluate the committee's work.
• See that the chairperson and the committee get the proper information and assignments.
• See that the committee meets regularly and reports to the church.

In most cases where staff advisors are used, the pastor works with the various staff members to coordinate the total committee effort.

Some churches use a committee on committees to coordinate committee work. This committee has responsibility for selecting and electing committee members. It also has the added responsibility of seeing that committees meet, perform their duties, and report to the church.

As indicated before, some churches use the Church Leadership Team to coordinate committee work. Some churches work through the deacons to coordinate committee work. A deacon is assigned to each committee. These deacons have similar responsibilities to those of the staff advisors previously mentioned.

Every church should evaluate and establish a method of committee coordination. To leave it to chance will cause many problems. The decision may sound simple, but establishing a method of coordination will eliminate many committee problems in churches.

Committee coordination is not something a committee may choose to do or not to do. Churches that are serious in planning for coordination will most likely have successful committee work.

One of the most popular axioms in the business world is Murphy's Law, "If anything can go wrong, it will." Perhaps this applies to committee work more than anywhere else, especially to committee work that has no coordination.

Chapter 7

COMMITTEE TRAINING AND ORIENTATION

Committee training should include an overview of the job description. If a printed job description is not available, the committee on committees and/or nominating committee should work with the committee to develop one. If the job description was used to enlist committee members and their spiritual gifts line up with the overall work of the committee, the job description then becomes a guide to more effective individual work.

Another element of training is orientation. Committee orientation can be led by the staff and committee on committees or nominating committee or by individual committee chairpersons.

Training for new committee members also involves reading previous years' minutes. Minutes help put in context the committee's job description and provide valuable information about how the committee has functioned in the past. Committee minutes usually provide future direction and research basic to a committee's work.

A church can involve its committee members in orientation in two ways: the single-session orientation plan or the dual-session plan. These sessions provide orientation to committee members regarding their duties and the initial planning for each committee.

Single-Session Orientation Plan

In the single-session orientation plan committees meet at the same time, called or convened by the chairperson of the nominating committee or the staff member who may have responsibility for working with the nominating committee.

All committee members, especially those rotating onto committees, should be provided a committee manual that gives them basic information regarding the committee. The committee manual should include such information as a committee roster, purpose statement for the committee, minutes of the previous year's meetings, a job description, and policies and procedures related to the committee.

As the orientation session begins, the nominating committee chairperson or responsible staff member should begin the meetings by discussing briefly the church's mission and its current year's goals. Then the pastor should lead all committee members in a time of motivation and inspiration that focuses on the importance of their involvement in the work of the church through its committees.

After the general session, each committee should meet separately. The orientation should continue with a standard agenda developed for committee chairpersons to use in the first meeting. The chairperson should convene the meeting, leading off with icebreakers, making sure everyone on the committee knows one another.

The chairperson should then focus the committee's attention on the current year's assignments. The chairperson also should describe how the previous year's work helped the church accomplish its goals. New committee members should have an opportunity to ask questions about the committee's work and discuss the committee's relationship to the church's mission and to other committees. Before the next meeting, new members should have an opportunity to review the previous year's work of the committee. More questions can be asked in the next meeting, providing ongoing orientation.

As the orientation session progresses, the committee chairperson should discuss the following with all the members: meeting times, the importance of agendas, opportunities for input beyond regular meeting times, and the importance of their role as committee members. This segment should provide a clear indication that their part in doing the work of the church through this committee is essential for the church to function at its best.

If time permits and the church has a place large enough, all committee members should reconvene for a 35-to 40-minute session. This session provides each committee chairperson an opportunity to make a brief statement, sharing with all other committees an overview of his or her committee's proposed work.

Reporting provides an opportunity for new members to understand their assignments for the new year and provides accountability for the committee and chairperson.

Following the reporting time, the pastor should lead in a prayer for wisdom and insight as committee members do their job to help the church reach its goals in the coming year.

Two-Session Orientation Plan

The two-session orientation plan provides more time for the orientation and calls for more specific training opportunities. The first session could be specifically for committee chairpersons and should be led by the pastor, responsible staff member, or an outside trainer. The second session should be for all committee members and should be led by the committee chairperson. The schedule for these two sessions should allow enough time for both groups to receive what is needed to perform their duties appropriately.

This orientation should begin with a how-to session describing the role of the chairperson in developing more effective committees. Some of the how-tos covered in this session could be developing agendas, identifying and working with learning styles of members, making arrangements for committee meetings, keeping effective records, and developing reporting methods that keep the congregation informed.

Following the how-to session, each chairperson should make a brief statement of purpose to the entire group. This process helps chairpersons focus more intentionally on their particular committees, building mutual accountability for the church's work. This process also can inspire committee chairpersons to encourage one another.

The second session should be an orientation session for new members, initiating group-building processes and establishing standards for the work of the committee. Each committee should meet separately with its new committee members.

A committee manual can be used to expedite this orientation. A committee manual contains the committee roster, purpose statement of the committee, job description, minutes of the previous year's meetings, and completed actions from the last several years.

The chairperson should clarify the purpose of the committee and relate that purpose to the church's mission and current yearly goals. Then members, especially new committee members, can begin to evaluate the committee's work and their particular assignments.

A statement should be developed that will serve as a mission statement for a new committee. An opportunity to share that statement with the other committees should be provided at the closing session. The statement could be written on an overhead cel and then discussed briefly.

As the committees are called back into a general session, each committee chairperson should introduce the new committee members rotating onto the committee and share the committee's mission statement and goals for the coming year. This presentation, as in the single-session orientation plan, should provide an opportunity for committee members to clarify their goals for the year and to establish accountability with the church for pursuing their individual work.

Special Committee Orientation Plan

These two orientation plans generally cover all the orientation needs that standing or permanent committees in the church need. Special committees need as much orientation as standing committees.

Generally, when a special committee is called into service, its purpose is for a particular reason and should be described in the church's bylaws or organization manual. If a chairperson and members are appointed for this special committee, their work should be specifically described, and any orientation needed should relate specifically to how the group would accomplish its specific assignment.

The special committee should establish a meeting time, and the committee chairperson should develop an agenda that would sustain the work of the committee through its meetings.

Special committees function, report their findings or recommendations, and go out of existence.

Chapter 8

THE ROLE
OF THE CHAIRPERSON

Knowing the duties of a committee chairperson can help the chairperson have a good committee experience. Perhaps each church will have varying responsibilities for its committee chairpersons, but some responsibilities are common.

Understand the Committee's Duties

A chairperson should understand the job he has accepted. For the chairperson to understand his job, he must have a committee job description. To understand the history of the committee, he would also need the records of past meetings, reports, and recommendations.

The chairperson should also talk with the pastor or staff member who is responsible for committee work. In this talk the chairperson should seek to discover such things as
- why the committee was formed
- when the committee was formed
- problems the committee might be facing
- interpretation of the policies and procedures related to this committee's work
- relationship of this committee to the church, Church Leadership Team, deacons, church officers, and other committees

Material or articles on group dynamics and team building will provide a committee chairperson with helpful information to guide the work of a committee.

Communicate Committee Responsibilities

Once the chairperson understands the job, she should plan to lead committee members to know and understand their duties as individuals and as a committee. Committee members must know what their job is. They should have been informed of the nature of the committee and its work as they were being enlisted, but greater understanding comes about by attending an orientation. If the chairperson takes time to interpret the information he has discovered about the committee and its history, he will help the committee members do a better job.

As soon as possible after the committee has been elected, the chairperson should plan an orientation meeting for the committee. In some churches, all committees are given orientation at one time. The purpose should be to discuss and clarify any questions committee members have concerning the committee's duties. (See chapter 7.)

Before orientation, the chairperson should secure and distribute copies of the committee's duties as well as copies of the church committee policies and procedures. The chairperson should suggest that each member study the duties carefully and explain that at the orientation meeting the committee will discuss the job description and will review minutes of previous meetings.

The chairperson should review expectations for committee members. Meeting these expectations will demonstrate commitment to the responsibility they have assumed.

- *Focus on the agenda.* The agenda becomes a guide for their involvement. They should study the agenda before the meeting and organize their thoughts related to individual issues. They also should be prepared to carry out individual assignments in a timely manner.
- *Practice effective church membership.* Be involved in Bible study and other activities of the church regularly.
- *Attend meetings.* Arrive 15 minutes early, or at least on time.
- *Study, pray, communicate, influence others, and engage in hard decisions.*
- *Protect the confidentiality of the committee's work.*

The role of a committee member and the role of a committee chairperson are important. Both are needed to produce effective committee work. Committee meetings are only as effective as the people who participate in them.

Understand Committee Members

The chairperson should build and develop relationships with committee members. Committee members bring a variety of personality styles to meetings. These styles impact others and relate to taking charge, influencing decisions, allowing change, wearing their feelings on their sleeves, or wanting to stay with the status quo.

Probably the most important action a committee chairperson can take is to become familiar with the learning styles of the individual members of the committee. Many chairpersons think they know everybody well and forge full-scale into a committee meeting without taking into consideration the differences that exist among individual committee members. A committee chairperson will encourage and receive participation from individual committee members more effectively if he practices a sensitivity to differences existing among people .

This sensitivity regarding individual members can be developed by using personality profiles or by asking questions such as: How do you process information? Do you think about it before you decide? Do you decide and then feel?

Responses to such questions or information gained from personality profiles help the committee chairperson make better decisions regarding the introduction of information, group discussion, and member responses before or after the meetings. The chairperson can take actions to help members make better decisions. For instance, if one committee member tends to react emotionally when new information is introduced, the chairperson could give committee members the information several days before the meeting and encourage them to become familiar with it before the meeting. This process prepares the one committee member who might react emotionally to newly introduced information and can help generate discussion by other committee members.

Plan Committee Meetings

The most important phase of good committee work is planning good committee meetings. The amount of time spent planning a meeting should be commensurate with the job to be done. A committee chairperson who neglects planning for effective meetings commits the unpardonable sin in committee work. Good planning requires at minimum five actions.

Determine the purpose of the meetings. The chairperson should state the purpose of the meeting before she even begins to plan the details of the meeting. The purpose should be stated in the form of a goal. Fore example: "The purpose of this meeting is to formulate and recommend policies concerning the use of buildings and facilities by church and outside groups."

Stating the purpose of the meeting has several advantages. One advantage is that it sets the limits of the meeting. The chairperson or members can tell when they begin "chasing rabbits" if the purpose is clearly understood. A purpose also helps determine the time needed for the meeting. Finally, a purpose gives the committee direction. A purpose becomes a goal in this case. When the goal is achieved, the committee can take pride in its accomplishments.

Some suggestions for purposes include:
- receiving reports from committee members on assignments that have been made
- defining analyzing, or solving a problem
- sharing information on a particular subject
- reconciling differing views

Schedule the meeting. The chairperson should follow the church's procedure in scheduling committee meetings. To schedule a meeting the chairperson should check with the office that maintains the calendar for the church. Scheduling the meeting through the church will help eliminate any duplications of meetings or conflicts with other church activities.

Prepare an agenda. An agenda serves as a guideline to move a committee toward accomplishing its purpose. Using an agenda develops participation and eliminates misunderstandings. The purpose of the meeting should dictate the agenda. Most agendas have the following elements:
- date, place, time of meeting
- subject(s) for discussion
- background statements
- present condition of subject
- purpose and aim of meeting

Committee members work better when an agenda is provided them at least three to five days prior to the meeting. Committee members should seek clarification concerning unclear information prior to the meeting time. Using an agenda allows committee members to have adequate time to react and respond to issues. Providing committee members time to work through issues prior to the meeting saves group time in processing emotional reactions. Energy is directed toward the committee's assignment.

Notify members. The committee should be notified as early as possible about the meeting date and time. The chairperson should work with the committee secretary and the church secretary to remind members of the meeting and their particular assignments. The notice should indicate the location of the meeting and the time the meeting will end. All the necessary information should be given to committee members in this notification.

Prepare the meeting room. Facilities go a long way toward determining the success of a meeting. Not just any room will do. In one church the deacons met in an auditorium that seated 250 people. The most present for any deacons meeting was 30 to 35. This environment did not lend itself to group discussions.

The room arrangement must also be conducive to a committee meeting. Preferably the room should have a table and a sufficient number of chairs for committee members.

The meeting room should be well-lighted. Proper heating, cooling, and ventilation are also important to the functioning of the committee. Physical discomfort can affect the participation of committee members.

A table enhances a committee meeting if group discussion and group work are required. If committee members are expected to write and/or take notes, a table is a must. Other items of equipment needed may include chalkboard, chalk, pencils, paper, and visual-aid equipment such as posters and poster stands.

Note the illustration below that shows the table arrangement with persons seated around the table, enabling committee members to communicate with everyone present.

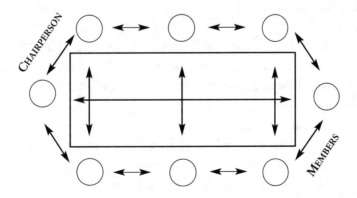

Lead Committee Meetings

A committee chairperson is judged by how he leads meetings. Several suggestions will help the committee chairperson be more effective in leadership.

Premeeting suggestions. Before the meeting begins, the chairperson should arrive early and arrange the room. If the meeting requires equipment, such as an overhead projector, the chairperson should arrive early enough to set up and test the projector.

The heating/air conditioning should be checked to be sure it is working properly. Materials that need to be distributed should be set at every place. The agenda should be placed at every chair; even though it may have been mailed earlier, the chairperson should always have copies available at the meeting. Pencil and paper should be provided for each person. Refreshments should be planned if the meeting will be lengthy.

Start on time. Consider this scenario: *A chairperson called a meeting of the planning and survey committee for 7:00 p.m. At 7:00 p.m. several committee members were present, including the chairperson. A representative from a consulting firm was present to present plans plans for remodeling facilities. The minutes seemed to drag by. At approximately 7:15 the chairperson said, "Welcome, I think everybody is here. We can begin." During the break one member of the committee told another member that he had driven faster than the speed limit to get back from a business appointment to this meeting that was supposed to begin at 7:00 p.m.*

Mark it down! Start the meeting at the stated time to begin. A chairperson is unfair to people who get to a meeting on time if she waits for latecomers. Fellowship is important, but unless the agenda is structured to have a period of fellowship at the beginning, start the meeting at the designated time.

Conduct a review of the agenda. At the beginning of the meeting the chairperson should remind the committee about the agenda for the meeting. The chairperson should highlight the topics to be discussed. Following a review of the agenda, the chairperson should call on someone to pray for God's leadership related to the agenda items.

Work through the agenda items. The agenda should be structured so that the most important and most pressing matters are dealt with first. Treating the most important items first ensures that only the least important items will be left if time runs out.

Involve all members. A chairperson can do many things to get committee members involved. However, he should be careful not to use manipulation. The chairperson should let committee members know that he wants their involvement and should use certain techniques that will get them involved. The suggestions offered here are only starters. The resourceful chairperson can find additional methods.

- *Distribute appropriate information/reports prior to the meeting.* By distributing this information prior to the meeting, people will be more ready to participate. If committee members have not heard of the topic to be discussed or if they have no information on the topic, they are often reluctant to offer their opinions.
- *Ask open-ended questions.* An open-ended question requires more than a yes or no answer. The person who answers this type of question must do some reflective thinking. An example of an open-ended question is, What can our church do to increase the number of tithers?

- *Ask questions to individuals.* The chairperson may ask the question to the entire committee, or she may direct the question to an individual who is not participating in the discussion. However, she should be careful about asking questions to specific individuals and be sensitive to a person's understanding, personality, and needs. Some individuals may be embarrassed if they are not able to provide answers. The chairperson can determine their feelings by talking to committee members ahead of time. He should ask if he could call on them for specific suggestions. He may want to give those persons the questions he is going to ask prior to the meeting. They will be able to do their homework and to answer the questions.
- *Use the brainstorming approach.* The brainstorming approach is one of the most successful ways of getting people involved. Brainstorming elicits the creative ideas of people in relation to a topic. The idea behind brainstorming is to get as many ideas from people as possible. No criticism is allowed, and no one can object initially to any idea presented. After many ideas are contributed, refinement can begin on them.

J. Ralph Hardee offered seven tips for facilitating committee member involvement in the August 1987 issue of *Church Administration.*

1. Recognize and affirm both the present and potential contribution(s) of each member present. A rule of thumb: call every person by name at least once during the course of the meeting.
2. Elicit ideas and opinions from each member.
3. Listen carefully to comments, rebuttals, and questions offered by members and clarify issues and ideas so that everyone understands them.
4. Encourage an open sharing of views. Show respect for all ideas and viewpoints expressed. Strive for total impartiality when responding to ideas and opinions.
5. Permit everyone who wants to participate in a discussion to speak at least once before anyone speaks a second time.
6. Restate conclusions reached and assignments made.
7. Alter the pace and tone of the meeting to rekindle interest and to prevent drifting toward boredom. Varying the flow or focus of the meeting in midstream can affect positively the attention and energy level of the members. ... Break the tension by using humor, anecdotes, experiences, and/or illustrations with which members can identify.[1]

Stay on track. Most committee meetings that go astray or become ineffective are those in which the committee does not stay on track. The chairperson should not allow too much discussion related to nonagenda items.

For example, in one committee meeting, the discussion centered around the committee's work assignment of renovating the church property. Members strayed from the subject by talking about lack of funds. The committee spent 15 minutes discussing how money should be obtained for some expenditures. Not only was this subject covered by church policies and procedures, but it also was a nonagenda item. Time could have been saved if the chairperson had kept the committee on track.

How does a chairperson keep the meeting on track? The following suggestions are offered as possibilities;

- *Limit discussion to agenda items.* The chairperson will find keeping people from venturing off agenda items difficult, but he should develop the art of being able to bring the people back. He could say, "That is an interesting topic for discussion. I wonder if we might save it for a future meeting." Or he might say, "This discussion is not on our agenda for tonight. Perhaps we should plan another meeting at which time we could discuss this topic." Another method of handling discussion not related to the agenda would be, "These are interesting items to discuss, but they are not related to our present business. Perhaps if we move through the agenda, we will be able to discuss these items after the committee meeting is over."

  Of course, the chairperson must use tact and courtesy in dealing with this problem. She may help by forewarning members that if they get off the track she will ask them to hold the discussion for future meetings or for a fellowship time after the meeting.

- *Summarize key points.* When the discussion seems to be drifting away from the main agenda item, the chairperson may summarize what has been said up to this point. Begin by saying, "Let me see if I can summarize what has been said thus far." Using this technique keeps everybody interested and informed. This is an excellent technique to help those present see what has been achieved.

- *Use the problem-solving method.* The problem-solving method should save committee time. Problem solving involves identifying the problem, gathering and analyzing facts, identifying solutions, selecting the best solution, and implementing the solution.

- *Reach conclusions as soon as possible.* The way to stay on track is to push forward quickly to a conclusion. Ample time must be allowed for discussion, but always keep moving the committee toward a solution of the problem.

The committee chairperson should not let discussion continue if she senses the group is ready for a decision. In one planning retreat, committee members were planning objectives for an association. Several areas had been identified, and the chairperson wanted to make sure the people were satisfied. He kept coming back with the question, "Do you think these objectives are representative of our association?" After a few minutes of discussion, he asked it another way, "Do you think we have reached a decision on the objectives?" After a few more minutes of discussion, they were obviously ready to make a decision and move on.

Complete the meeting. Just as important as the way to start a meeting is the way to end a meeting. If the concluding time for the meeting has been established, the chairperson should be aware of what is happening and how close the group is to concluding the work to be done. Suppose the work has progressed properly. How can the chairperson close the meeting effectively?

1. *Review all decisions.* In most committee meetings several decisions have been made. The chairperson should review these decisions by reading them aloud, or he may choose to summarize without reading. Reviewing the decisions will provide the proper feedback to see if the committee is in agreement with decisions made. This method also enhances the communication process.

2. *Consider unsolved problems.* Often unsolved problems have to be considered. The chairperson should ask the committee to plan future meetings to work on these unresolved questions or problems. The chairperson needs to remember that the meeting should conclude at the time indicated. If the time to conclude the meeting has arrived and unfinished business remains, the chairperson should ask if the committee wants to continue discussion past the ending time or schedule another meeting.

3. *Make follow-up assignments.* For work that is incomplete, the chairperson needs to make assignments for future meetings. Committee members should be clear on their assignments and when their work is due. After the meeting the chairperson should make these assignments in writing and send them to committee members.

Follow Up on Committee Meetings

The meeting may be over, but the chairperson's job continues. As soon as possible after the meeting, he should take several actions.

1. *Follow up on the meeting minutes.* The chairperson and the secretary should go over the minutes to clarify any confusion that may exist. Copies of the minutes should be sent to all members, including the pastor or appropriate staff members. These minutes need to be available to committee members at least 48 hours following the meeting.

2. *Report regularly to the Church Leadership Team and/or church business meeting on committee activities.*

3. *Present committee recommendations to the Church Leadership Team, the church business meeting, or other appropriate groups.* The chairperson is responsible for providing material to the church moderator and the congregation. Any committee action should be given in writing to the church clerk; the action should be stated clearly and should be neatly written or typed. These recommendations become a part of the church's official minutes and therefore become a part of the church's legal documents.

4. *Receive progress reports from members on assigned activities.*

5. *Work with church staff members, church officers, Church Leadership Team, deacons, church ministry directors, and other committees.*

The role of a committee chairperson is strategic. This person does not do the work of the committee for the church. This person leads committee members to understand their work and to process individual differences so members have opportunity to be involved to the fullest extent of their gifts and strengths. The chairperson is significant because he can help provide a growth experience for individuals who serve.

---

[1]J. Ralph Hardee, "The Role of the Committee Chairperson," *Church Administration*, August 1987, 10.

Chapter 9

EFFECTIVE COMMITTEE WORK

Doctors prescribe medicine for an illness. In some cases therapy is required. But even after the diagnosis is made and the prescription is written, the doctor often says, "This should do it, but if you continue to have problems, I may have to change the prescription."

What the doctor is really saying is, "I believe I know what the problem is, and this medicine should make you well. But I can't guarantee success. I may have to try something else."

No one can guarantee success even if a prescribed set of rules and regulation is followed. But following a few guidelines can help churches have functioning, productive committees and avoid some of the pitfalls many churches have experienced.

ADOPT POLICIES AND PROCEDURES

Policies and procedures are necessary in any organization. A church has policies. They may be written or unwritten, but they are there. The same is true for procedures. Procedures are not always spelled out step-by-step, but every church follows certain procedures in its operations.

Policies

Policies are guidelines that establish the limits of an organization's work. Polices spell out rules and help identify the exceptions to the rules. They help church committees function properly by defining a standard method of operation.

Churches should consider writing policies in the following areas:

Classification of committees. This policy should state that all committees will be classified at the time they are established. When new committees are formed, they should be classified as regular/permanent or special/temporary.

Organization. This policy should explain how committees will be organized. Usually this will require a chairperson, vice chairperson, secretary, and a certain number of members.

Selection and election. This policy should state how committee members are selected and elected.

Rotation. A policy relating to rotation of committee members is needed. Usually one-third of the committee members rotate off each year. Rotation is discussed in a further section of this chapter.

Vacancies. A policy needs to be written concerning how vacancies will be filled. In some churches a committee on committees has this responsibility. Other churches have the nominating committee to fulfill this role.

Meetings. A policy should state the frequency of meetings. Committees do not all need to meet the same number of times. But all committees should meet during the year.

Budgeting. Many committees have responsibility for preparing a budget request each year. A policy is needed to tell how committees relate to the budget planning process. For example, a policy statement could read: "All regular committees should submit requests for budget monies to the stewardship committee during budget planning time."

Purchasing or expending monies. All committees should abide by the church policy on expenditures of funds.

Reports. A policy statement should reflect the need for committees to report to the congregation.

Minutes. Committees need to keep accurate minutes of meetings. A policy statement should reflect this requirement.

A set of policies related to committee work may include other areas. These seem to be the most important. However, each church must consider its committee work and write policies necessary to help committees function smoothly and efficiently.

Procedures

Policies state what the rules are. Procedures tell how to carry out the rules. A church should consider developing procedures for several functions of committee life. The following suggestions may help.

Election. One church uses the following procedure for committee election:
- Each year the pastor will appoint, with approval of the church, the chairperson of the committee on committees.
- The newly appointed chairperson, with the help of the pastor, will select eight committee members.
- The chairperson of the committee on committees will present the slate of committee members to the church for approval.
- The committee on committees will disband after the election of committee members.

Budgeting. If the policy related to budgeting requires that all committees submit budget requests to the budget planning committee or stewardship committee, the following procedures may make that process work smoothly.
- Committees meet in August and September to plan projects for the new year of work. (The months may change depending on your church's budgeting calendar.)
- Committees plan projects and activities and suggest budgeted amounts for them.
- Committees submit budget requests to the budget planning or stewardship committee in October or the appropriate month.

Reports. Procedures should be spelled out for committees to make reports. Do committees make the reports directly to the church? If so, do they give copies to the church office, church clerk, or someone else? Does the chairperson keep copies of these reports? The procedures for making reports, giving reports, and filing reports should be spelled out clearly.

Vacancies. The step-by-step process of how vacancies need to be filled should be defined carefully. One example of a procedure for filling vacancies follows.

- Committee chairperson reports the loss of a committee member to the appropriate group (committee on committees, nominating committee, Church Leadership Team, or deacons). If a committee coordinator is used, the chairperson will report this loss to the committee coordinator.
- The appropriate person or group takes action to enlist and nominate a replacement.
- The nominating group presents the newly enlisted committee member(s) to the church for election.
- The chairperson invites the newly elected committee member(s) to the next regular meeting of the committee.

These are only examples of procedures. Your church will need to write committee procedures that follow normal church procedures.

WRITE JOB DESCRIPTIONS

Many committees flounder because they do not know their jobs. Having committees without job descriptions is like having a trip with no ultimate destination. Committee job descriptions are merely a list of duties.

Written job duties prevent buck passing. When duties are clearly defined, committees and committee members know their responsibilities. A statement of job duties provides boundaries for the committee's work. Job descriptions set the limits of how far a committee can go. Job descriptions can also be used as evaluation instruments.

The following suggestions will help in writing committee duties.

Determine which committees are needed. Often a church has more committees than it needs. Suggestions have been given in previous chapters concerning how to determine which committees may be needed.

Assign the responsibility for writing duties. Asking a committee to write duties in one of its meetings will present an impossible task. Assignments should be made to committee members prior to the meeting. If a church has sufficient staff, a staff member could write the first draft of committee duties and present it to the committee for evaluation and rewriting.

Present the proposed job duties to the total committee for study. Once the duties have been written by various committee members or staff members, the entire list should be presented to the total committee for study. Sufficient time needs to be given to committee members for this study. Do not present the duties in a committee meeting and expect members to approve those duties in the same meeting.

Revise the duties as necessary. When all the duties are presented, the committee may discover some overlapping and duplication. Committee members should feel the freedom to make changes at this point.

Adopt a statement of duties for each committee. The committee should reach a conclusion and recommendation related to the statement of duties.

Present duties for each committee to the congregation. When presenting the duties to the congregation, allow sufficient time to study the duties. The church should have a minimum of a month to study the duties of all committees before being asked to vote.

Ask the congregation to adopt the statement of duties. This adoption should take place in a regular business meeting or called business meeting. If it is a called business meeting, the congregation should be notified about the purpose of the meeting. When the duties are adopted, they become the official statement of duties for each committee.

USE THE ROTATION SYSTEM

Many churches have found that the rotation system improves the overall effectiveness of committee work. However, the rotation system has advantages and disadvantages. A church needs to study the system carefully if it is not currently being used.

Consider some of the disadvantages. For example, good committee members rotate off if the system is followed. Some churches prefer to keep good committee members for an indefinite period of time. Smaller-membership churches often find that they do not have enough people to implement the rotation system.

Another problem related to the rotation system involves the chairperson. If careful attention is not give to the selection process, a committee may find itself with an inexperienced chairperson. Placing qualified committee members on the committees provides the answer to this dilemma.

Resignations also provide some problems with the rotation system. A committee member may resign before the term of service is expired. Policies need to provide for replacing this person.

Advantages of the Rotation System

In most situations, the rotation system has many advantages that outweigh the disadvantages. Consider the following advantages of the rotation system.

Uses resources wisely. A church has great resources in its members. Using people where their talents and skills can make a maximum contribution will make the church more effective in its ministry. Rotation of committee members enhances these possibilities. Most churches have members who are willing to serve on committees. If the rotation system is not used, many of these people will never get the opportunity to serve on committees.

Allows different members to serve as chairperson. Often committee members will accept the responsibility of serving as chairperson if they know the assignment will last for only one or two years. And no person should be asked to serve as chairperson the first year she serves on a committee. Conversely, the rotation system prohibits any one person from gaining control of a certain area of church life or becoming too powerful. This principle becomes important when considering such areas as finance and personnel.

Aids nominating/enlisting group. When the rotation system is used, all committee members are not replaced every year. This makes the work of the nominating group much easier. In most cases, only one-third of a committee's members need to be replaced each year.

Removes ineffective members. Ineffective members often are the result of a person serving in the wrong position. The member might be too embarrassed to admit the problem. Rotation will eliminate the ineffective member.

Setting Up a Rotation System

The key to an effective rotation system involves a good start. If your church considers starting the rotation system, several suggestions might help. First, begin early discussing the possibilities. Asking the church to adopt the rotation system without prior discussion is not advisable. Discuss the system—what it is and how it works—with the appropriate groups. The Church Leadership Team, the deacons, the committees—all of these groups may need to be included in the discussion. If needed, discussion could take as long as a year before asking the church to adopt the system.

A church should consider appointing a special committee to study the rotation system and bring a recommendation to the congregation. This special committee could do some of the following:

- Survey other churches of like size to determine whether the rotation system is used and the advantages or disadvantages these churches can identify.
- Study the advantages and disadvantages. This book can serve as a resource.
- Talk with church members to discover feeling and thoughts. A word of caution: Don't expect too many positive responses if this is a new concept to your congregation.
- Talk with denominational leaders. Often these leaders have served effectively in churches. They can possibly shed some light on the system.
- Prepare a written report to the congregation along with the recommendations.

If the committee recommends that the church adopt the rotation system, the recommendation should include implementation procedures. Items to be considered in implementing the rotation system include the date for the process to begin, who will have responsibility for implementing the process, how present committee members will be assigned terms of service, and what the term of service will be for newly elected committee members.

Most rotation systems use a three-year term of service. The number of committee members needs to be a multiple of three. The first year of implementation will require present members to be assigned a one-, two-, or three-year term. In subsequent years, new committee members will be assigned a three-year term unless a person is being nominated to fill a vacancy.

When the committees are presented for election, indicating the term of service could eliminate some confusion. For example:

Term ends	9/30/03	9/30/04	9/30/05
	Rex Lee, Chairperson	Mary Taylor	James Neushafer
	Ann Edwards*	Ken Mead	Bettie Hagan

*Filling a 1-year vacancy

REPORT TO THE CONGREGATION

Since church committees are elected by the congregation, committees should report to the congregation because it has a right to know what the committees are doing toward accomplishing their duties. Also, regular reporting encourages a spirit of achievement. When a committee makes regular reports, the congregation becomes enthusiastic about the accomplishments.

Most church members like to know the church's needs, problems, and opportunities. Regular reporting improves and enhances communication to the congregation. Reporting can also serve as an evaluation tool. Some person or group should periodically evaluate the effectiveness of committee work. Specific results as reported by committees will enable the evaluation process to be more effective.

A committee can report in several ways. Verbal reporting can cause negative reactions and feelings. The probability of church members' misunderstanding a report is increased if the report is given only verbally.

The following suggestions may improve the reporting process by church committees.

Visual Methods

Visuals add a great deal to reports. People often remember more of what they see than what they hear. Several options are available for using visuals. Charts and graphs are helpful for presenting statistical data.

Pictures, slides, videos, or multimedia presentations often enhance the reporting process. For example, your church may be considering the need for a renovation project for some of its facilities. A video or slides that show cracked walls, peeling paint, and stained ceilings could convince the congregation more quickly than just stating that renovation is necessary.

Another method of visual reporting is the bulletin board. Some churches use this technique in reporting mission trips, camping experiences, or other trips. Color photos are posted on the appropriate bulletin board, providing a visual report to the congregation.

Panel Methods

Panel symposiums and panel discussions offer excellent opportunities to improve reporting. The stewardship committee or budget planning committee could use a panel to present the proposed budget to the congregation. Program leaders, staff members, and committee chairpersons could serve on the panel to present and interpret various sections of the budget. After the presentation, the congregation could ask questions of the panel members for further clarification.

Written Reports

In most cases, a written report or recommendation should accompany a verbal or visual report. Church members need something to read or to take home for additional study. Without a written report, members have to rely on memory, causing a possible information gap.

LIMIT COMMITTEE SIZE

Keep committee membership as small as possible. The number of committee members should relate to the committee duties. How many committee members are necessary to do the work? For example, if the flower committee has only the responsibility of soliciting persons to provide flowers for the sanctuary, three people may handle this task without overworking any one person. On the other hand, the stewardship committee may have four subsections. As many as twelve people may serve on this committee.

Another factor that needs to be considered is the size of the church. Smaller-membership churches may not have enough people to place more than three on each committee. Larger-membership churches obviously can involve more people in the work of the church by increasing the number of committee members.

USE EFFECTIVE ENLISTMENT PROCEDURES

The telephone rings at Mr. Stewart's home. "Mr. Stewart, this is Joe McMillan from the church. Listen, the nominating committee is here at the church. We're trying to get our committees together for next year. We have to present all the names to the church next Wednesday night. Will you serve on the property and space committee?"

Mr. Stewart responds, "Well, I don't know. Tell me. What does this committee do?"

Mr. McMillan says, "I'm not really sure. I believe they look out after all our buildings or something like that. But, I know you can do the job. Will you?"

Mr. Stewart asks, "How often does the committee meet?"

Mr. McMillan replies, "Oh, I don't know. Not much. They don't do a whole lot that I know of. I'm sure you would have the time to give this committee. Will you do it?"

If you had to guess how this conversation ended, do you think Mr. Stewart said yes or no? Probably he said no, not because he wasn't willing to serve, but because the enlistment process failed.

Following are suggestion for selecting, enlisting, and electing committee members.

Selecting and Nominating Committee Members

Who is responsible for selecting and nominating committee members? Some churches allow the nominating committee to nominate committee members. Other churches use a committee on committees. Often, the determining factor involves the work load of the nominating committee. In smaller-membership churches, the number of people to be enlisted in ministry organizations does not overwhelm the nominating committee. In this situation, the nominating committee could manage enlistment of committee members.

Larger-membership churches require more volunteers for their ministry organizations. In these churches, a committee on committees might prove helpful. Often larger churches also have more committees than smaller-membership churches. This makes using a committee on committees practical.

How do you find people to serve on committees? Committee members should be selected on the basis of their spiritual gifts. Spiritual gift inventories enable the nominating committee or the committee on committees to make the best selection.

Another method involves a talent search. Prepare a list of committees with descriptive statement(s) about the purpose of each committee. Distribute this list and ask church members to indicate the committee(s) on which they would like to serve.

Another method requires the nominating group to search the church membership rolls for prospective committee members. Still another method involves the nominating group approaching other church leaders, such as Sunday School teachers, and asking them to recommend prospective committee members.

One of the dangers involved in selecting committee members is that often the same people are asked to serve as committee members. The nominating group should make every effort to discover and involve different people on committees.

Enlisting Committee Members

A church should be just as diligent about enlisting committee members as it is in enlisting Sunday School or other ministry leaders. Sound enlistment procedures require diligent effort and a lot of time. The enlistment process should be preceded by sincere prayer. The nominating group should pray together during the selection process and the enlistment process. Before approaching a person to ask her to serve on a committee, the enlister should spend time in prayer. Beyond praying, certain enlistment principles and procedures will enable the nominating group to be more effective in the enlistment process. These suggestions relate to enlisting new committee members.

Enlist face-to-face. The best enlistment process requires face-to-face conversation. A person can say no on the telephone easily. Also, if you are looking at a person as you try to enlist him, you can read body language. A face-to-face encounter highlights the importance of the work.

Call for an appointment. If the enlistment is done face-to-face, the enlister should make an appointment to visit with the prospective committee member. The visit can take place in the home, on the job, at the church, over a cup of coffee or lunch, or in a variety of other places. Setting a definite time also highlights the importance of the committee work.

Share and explain committee duties. The enlister should have a copy of the committee duties to share with the prospective committee member. The enlister should be familiar with committee duties so he can explain them to the prospect. If a prospective committee member does not understand the duties of the committee, she may be reluctant to say yes.

Have appropriate information. The enlister also should have other information that will be helpful to the prospective committee member. Several items of relevant information include

- the name of the chairperson
- the frequency of committee meetings
- any current projects in which the committee is involved
- the tenure of service (one year, two years, three years, or indefinite)

Allow time for the prospect to consider the request. In most cases the enlister should allow time for the prospect to pray and consider the request to serve. In some cases, the prospect may say yes immediately. The enlister should be sensitive to the prospect at this point and allow him to consider the request. The enlister should set a definite time to call the person to get an answer. The enlister could say, "May I call you next Sunday to get an answer? However, if you need additional information, don't hesitate to call me before then. My telephone number is _____."

Follow up as promised. If the enlister has given a deadline for an answer, she should follow up as promised. The follow-up work could be done by telephone. Visiting with the person face-to-face for a follow-up conversation is not necessary.

Electing Committee Members

The total enlistment process involves the election of committee members. Most churches require the congregation to elect committee members. Since church committees do administrative work for the congregation, electing committee members by the congregation naturally follows.

Several suggestions will enhance the election process. Follow the same procedures for electing committee members as used in electing ministry leaders.

Consider printing a list of committees and committee members for presentation to the congregation. Distributing this list widely in advance of voting at the business meeting would be helpful and informative. Embarrassing situations can be avoided if the committee list is printed early. On more than one occasion, a person has stood in a business meeting to say that he had not volunteered to serve on a committee or to say, "You misspelled my name."

Selecting, enlisting, and electing committee members requires careful attention by the nominating group. Perhaps these suggestions will make this process more effective. At least you may avoid the scenario described at the beginning of this section.

PERSONAL LEARNING ACTIVITIES

Chapter 1

1 Write the definition of a church committee as given in this chapter. Write your own definition.
2. Write one illustration from your experience that shows the need for church committees.
3. What are some benefits of using committees other than those listed in this chapter?

Chapter 2

1. List and explain the two types of committees suggested in this chapter.
2. List three criteria a church may use to determine what committees it needs.
3. In your church, what is the relationship of committees to the following groups?
Write a descriptive statement(s) for each one.
   - Pastor and staff
   - Church Leadership Team
   - Deacons
   - Other committees and/or councils
   - Congregation
4. List the steps suggested in this chapter to help a church establish its committee structure.

Chapter 3

1. List the four church officers mentioned in this chapter.
2. List and explain the responsibilities of the following officers:
   - Moderator
   - Church clerk
   - Church treasurer
   - Trustees
3. Discuss who should serve as moderator.
4. Give the definition of a trustee.

Chapter 4

1. Define permanent committee.
2. List from this book the suggested permanent committees and give a short description of each.
3. Obtain a list of committees your church uses. Compare the list with the suggested committee list from this book. Does your church have additional committees? Explain their functions. Are there committees your church does not have but perhaps needs to add? If yes, name the committee needed and why they are needed.

Chapter 5

1. Define special committee.
2. List some suggested special committees.
3. Define councils.
4. Explain briefly the need for special committees and councils.
5. Give examples of how your church uses special committees and councils.

Chapter 6

1. Write a definition of coordination.
2. Write one illustration from your experience that shows the need for coordinating committee work.
3. List the committee activities in a church that need to be coordinated.
4. List the four principles of coordination suggested in this chapter.
5. List the suggested methods of coordination found in this chapter.
6. Select the method of coordination you feel is best and state the reason(s) why.

Chapter 7

1. List the items to be covered in committee orientation.
2. Discuss the orientation for special committees.

Chapter 8

1. List the general duties of a committee chairperson.
2. List the five actions necessary for planning good committee meetings.
3. List the suggestions for leading committee meetings.
4. List the suggestions for involving committee members in a meeting.
5. Discuss the suggestions for keeping members on track during a committee meeting.

Chapter 9

1. Define policies and procedures.
2. Define job descriptions as the term relates to committees.
3. List the steps a church can follow to write committee job descriptions.
4. List the advantages and disadvantages of using the rotation system for committees.
5. Describe the three types of reporting suggested in this chapter.

SUGGESTIONS FOR THE TEACHER

Chapter 1

1. Share and discuss the definition of a church committee as stated in this chapter.
2. Lead the group to write its own definition of a church committee.
3. Prepare a chart or overhead transparency listing the benefits of church committees. Discuss these benefits at length. Ask group members to add to the list.

Chapter 2

1. Lead the group to discuss the two types of committees suggested in this chapter.
2. Make a sentence strip chart of the criteria used to determine a church's committee structure. Discuss these criteria with the group.
3. Lead the group to discuss the relationship of committees in your church to the various groups suggested in this chapter.

Chapter 3

1. Make a sign for each of the four church officers. Attach these signs to the walls of the room. Divide participants into four groups. Using the information in the chapter, ask each group to list on a sheet of newsprint the responsibilities of the church officers.
2. Allow each group to report on the responsibilities of the church officer assigned.

Chapter 4

1. Secure a list of the church's committees with description of responsibilities, and duplicate this list for each participant.
2. Thirteen committees are recommended in this book as permanent committees. Assign each participant one of the committees. If there are more than 13 participants divide persons into groups of two or three.
3. Ask each person to examine the responsibilities of the assigned committee. Examine the church committee list to see if that committee has been included. If it has, how do its responsibilities compare to the suggested responsibilities? If this committee has not been included in the past, is there a need for this committee to be added now? Why or why not?

Chapter 5

1. Ask two persons to serve on a panel to discuss the topic of special committees or councils. Each should be familiar with the information in chapter 5.
2. Allow all participants to question panel members about the responsibilities of special committees and councils.
3. Encourage participants to name the special committees and councils used by their church.

Chapter 6

1. Discuss the need for coordination by sharing some of the illustrations in this chapter. Add other illustrations from your experiences or experiences of the class.
2. Prepare a chart, an overhead transparency, or use the chalkboard to list the activities to be coordinated. Discuss these activities with the group.
3. Assign in advance to selected group members the various principles of coordination. Ask these group members to discuss the principle assigned to them at the appropriate time.

Chapter 7

1. Discuss the two orientation plans given in this chapter. Ask participants to give personal examples of positive and negative experiences in committee orientation.
2. Conclude with a discussion of items that need to be covered in committee orientation to ensure a meaningful experience for committee members.

Chapter 8

1. Prepare a chart or overhead cel of the general duties of committee chairpersons. Lead in a discussion of each duty.
2. When discussing the duty, "Planning Committee Meetings," list five elements of planning on a chalkboard or poster board. Discuss these elements.
3. Discuss the various parts of an agenda. Ask the group to plan a sample agenda.
4. When discussing the duty, "Leading Committee Members," be sure to include a discussion of how to involve committee members in the committee discussion.

Chapter 9

1. Make a chart listing the six major sections of the chapter. Use the chart to lead discussions of the various guidelines with material presented in this chapter.
2. Compile a statement of committee policies that your church has already adopted. Share these with the group and compare them with suggested policies in this chapter.
3. If your church has written job descriptions, secure copies and distribute to the group. Divide the group into two groups and ask them to discuss the following:
   Group 1: What are the disadvantages of the rotation system?
   Group 2: What are the advantages of the rotation system?